FIERCE

*I would like to dedicate this book to every
young woman who's ever felt lost*

FIERCE

KELLY OSBOURNE

2 4 6 8 10 9 7 5 3 1

Published in 2010 by Virgin Books, an imprint of Ebury Publishing
A Random House Group Company
First published in Great Britain by Virgin Books in 2009
This updated edition first published 2010

All photographs courtesy of Osbourne family archive unless otherwise stated
p.164 photograph © Silvia Mautner
p.232 photograph © Dave M. Bennett/Getty Images
p.250 photograph of Kelly in floppy hat © Mark Weiss

The information in this book has been compiled by way of general guidance in relation to
the specific subjects addressed, but is not a substitute and not to be relied on for medical,
pharmaceutical or other professional advice on specific circumstances and in specific locations.
Please consult your GP before changing, stopping or starting any medical treatment. So far as
the author is aware the information given is correct and up to date as at 2009. Practice, laws and
regulations all change, and the reader should obtain up-to-date professional advice on any such
issues. The author and publishers disclaim, as far as the law allows, any liability arising directly
or indirectly from the use, or misuse, of the information contained in this book.

The publisher has made serious efforts to trace the copyright owners of all photographs
reproduced in this book. Should any have inadvertently been overlooked the publisher would be
happy to acknowledge any rightful copyright owner and would be grateful for any information as
to their identity.

The Random House Group Limited Reg. No. 954009

Addresses for companies within the Random House Group can be found at
www.randomhouse.co.uk

A CIP catalogue record for this book is available from the British Library

The Random House Group Limited supports The Forest Stewardship Council [FSC],
the leading international forest certification organisation. All our titles that are printed
on Greenpeace-approved FSC-certified paper carry the FSC logo. Our paper procurement
policy can be found at www.rbooks.co.uk/environment

Mixed Sources
Product group from well-managed
forests and other controlled sources
www.fsc.org Cert no. TT-COC-2139
© 1996 Forest Stewardship Council
FSC

Text design: www.carrstudio.co.uk
Printed in the UK by CPI Bookmarque, Croydon CR0 4TD

ISBN 9780753519363

To buy books by your favourite authors and register for offers visit www.rbooks.co.uk

CONTENTS

PIPERS CORNER SCHOOL
1996

CHAPTER ONE

TURNING THIRTEEN

Parents are parents whether your father is a bank manager or a gardener. I found my dad embarrassing all the time.

Turning thirteen is the start of one of the hardest times of your entire life. It really is. You don't know who you are. You've got all these people telling you what's cool and what's not. There are just far too many influences in your life.

I had no idea what lay ahead when I celebrated my thirteenth birthday on 27 October 1997.

I expected that my life was going to change. Becoming a teenager was a big deal for me and I'd been looking forward to it. We were living at Welders. It's our family home in Buckinghamshire and it's where my parents live now when they're in the UK. Even though I've got my own home in London, Welders is the one place in the world where I feel really safe. I love that house so much. The special effects guy from *Star Wars* owned it before us. When I'm there I have the best night's sleep. Welders is hidden away on a leafy road.

You'd quite easily drive past it if you didn't know it was there.

It's probably not what you'd expect from our family, but it's homely and traditional. Mum's Mini Cooper sits outside and as soon as I open the door I know I'm home. Mum's put a lot of work into making it a family home and I see it as being really cosy. It's not a fancy house.

We've all made my mum and dad promise us they'll never sell it because it holds so many dear memories for all of us. It's surrounded by fields as far as the eye can see, full of deer and rabbits. When I look out of my bedroom window I feel so happy. My bedroom is still exactly the same as it was when we first moved there when I was nine. It's on the top floor, between my younger brother Jack's and my older sister Aimee's rooms.

My bedroom is girly. I wanted to be one of the boys, but deep down I secretly loved dolls and dresses. I really loved Peter Pan, but not in a Michael Jackson sort of way. My mum got a man to come in and paint a fairytale mural. It covers every wall with a huge beanstalk painted on one side. My whole family are characters painted on the walls too: there's me, my uncle Tony, who's not my real uncle but might as well be, my mum, dad, Jack and Aimee. I sat there on the floor among the paints, telling him exactly what to do.

My bathroom is pink and green. It still has the sponges spelling out my name sitting above the bath. I've never changed it. As a kid I was such a tomboy. I was obsessed with frogs. I really fucking loved frogs. My mum used to always go out and buy frog things for me. I don't know where she got them all from.

And there's a piece of Windsor Castle that I collected once, during a visit, in a cup sitting on top of the toilet. On the floor below, there's another bedroom I sometimes sleep in that's known as the Marilyn Monroe room with black and white pictures of her on the wall. I just think she embodies everything beauty is about. That woman died before her time. Every woman wishes they were like Marilyn – I do.

If you were to visit the house now, it's like we just picked up our stuff and left all those years ago when we moved to America not long after my thirteenth birthday. Everything is still in the same place, like our uniforms, games, clothes, toys – everything!

Outside our bedroom doors, the length of the landing, are white cupboards where my mum would keep our school uniforms and weekend clothes. My mum was always really concerned about our safety, and she had panic rooms built in the house in case intruders – who she referred to as the 'bad men' – broke in. The panic room was an area we could go to where we would be safe. It wasn't until we were older that we realised the people she was trying to protect us from were her father, my grandfather, Don Arden and his unsavoury entourage. My parents had a baseball bat by the side of their bed ready in case anyone broke in. And there was a knife under their mattress for a long time too.

WELDERS has always been a great home for a party. On my thirteenth birthday I had a fancy-dress-themed party. My birthday is near Halloween so that would happen a lot.

Everyone was invited. There were kids and adults and it was noisy and fun. I was excited.

I was a young thirteen. I mean, people in America still ID-check me now and I'm in my mid-twenties for fuck's sake. For the fancy dress, I wore a red wig, black Doc Marten boots, a black dress and white wings. I don't know what the fuck I was. I just thought I looked cool.

Gay cousin Terry's boyfriend came as Prince Charming and Mum dressed up as a nun. My mum, a bloody nun! Jack really didn't bother. He was wearing camouflage gear and a green baseball cap turned backwards. He was twelve and only interested in running around with the boys and singing on the karaoke machine. He stood there in his cute glasses clutching the microphone. I was so fucking jealous of those glasses because they made him look clever.

My dad wasn't on tour so it was one of the rare occasions he was there for my party, which made it even more fun. He kept popping in and out of the big tent that was in the garden at Welders, where the party was. It was huge and had a black dance floor. All my friends were there, including my best friends Fleur and Sammy. They're still my best friends today.

My mum knows how to throw a good party; it's her thing. She'd got in party organisers and caterers. There were balloons everywhere, kids running around and adults hanging out. There was a bloody DJ standing behind the decks playing requests.

As a kid, I used to be obsessed with this party entertainer called Ally Doolally: The Egyptian Magician. I'm not joking when I say I used to have him at every single birthday party. He

'*He was just standing* there in his underwear and *a military hat he'd found* somewhere in the house, then he started chasing everyone around singing the Backstreet Boys song *"Everybody".*'

always wore a brightly coloured turban and a gold genie outfit with a flowing cloak.

Ally was there, as usual, in the kitchen. It's open-plan and decorated in a very country cottage sort of way with a lounge area to one side and my dad's gym through into a back room. Ally – God, I loved him – did the best tricks and it was a really fun party.

And then Dad just kind of appeared from nowhere. He was absolutely shit-faced. Drunk. I'm talking really, really drunk. He was just standing there in his underwear and a military hat he'd found somewhere in the house, then he started chasing everyone around singing the Backstreet Boys song 'Everybody'.

At this point, I had a question. How the fuck did my dad know the words to that song? Fuck knows. But all my friends were screaming and running around the house. It was plain crazy. It was fucking fun. I mean, do I look like someone who'd have a normal birthday party?

One time, Dad dressed up as a werewolf at one of my parties, locked me and my friends up in the garden shed and then chased us all when we got out. My mum had to call everyone's parents because all the kids were crying and they all got collected and taken home.

People have often said to me, 'Oh it must have been so cool when you were growing up to have Ozzy Osbourne as your father.' People seem to think that because he's famous it means I never used to get embarrassed. But that's bullshit. Parents are parents whether your father is a bank manager or a gardener. I found my dad embarrassing all the time. All dads are embarrasing and (this might sound patronising but. . .) what I found humiliating then, I laugh about now – and you will too.

L ATER that evening, when my friends had all gone home, me and Jack went upstairs to check up on my dad. He had passed out on the bed, but our ex-nanny, who'd just come back for my party, was crawling on my parents' bedroom carpet on her hands and knees towards him saying, in this husky voice, 'Ozzy, I know you've always really wanted me.' She wanted to fuck him! Have you ever heard anything like it? My dad was oblivious – he'd passed out.

I think it was my uncle Tony who put her to bed. He's been my father's assistant since he was a teenager, when he used to follow Black Sabbath around.

While the nanny lay there out of it because she'd drunk too much, me and Jack began smearing Pedigree Chum dog food on her. Then we got bags of flour, an opened tin of baked beans and brown sauce that we'd taken from the kitchen and poured it all over her. My mum helped us. We were pissing ourselves laughing. Then Jack and I put cling film over the toilet seat so that if she needed to throw up during the night it'd go all over her too. She's known as 'the nanny who tried to fuck my dad'.

It never struck me at the time that it wasn't actually a normal thirteen-year-old's birthday party because it had an equal mix of adults and kids. And I was kind of hanging out with both of them. All the adults were going, 'Oh it's Ozzy, isn't he funny?' And so I convinced myself it was OK to think, 'Oh, Dad, aren't you funny?'

Turning Thirteen

M Y dad is a big kid, really. He'd always be coming out with the most crazy sayings like, 'Kelly, every action has a reaction.' Or another favourite was, 'You play. You pay.' As fucked up as he was at times, I count myself lucky to have my dad. There is only one Ozzy Osbourne.

Was I surprised that Dad had embarrassed me? No. I was used to it. It's the story of my life. Parents are there to embarrass you in front of your friends. My mum and dad have taken full advantage of this so-called 'privilege', I can tell you. I associate most major things that happened in my childhood and teenage years with being embarrassed by something my mum or dad have done.

I once suffered two major embarrassments in the space of two weeks! There was one time I'd come home from school one day and my mum had been to her favourite shop, Marks & Spencer. She'd left a pack of new knickers on my bed. I was so excited because I'd wanted these knickers for ages. They were really cute and had the days of the week written on the front. All the girls at school had them.

The next day I put a pair on. That night I brought all my friends back home from school and I was standing in the hallway. I bent down to put an exercise book in my backpack when my dad suddenly bellowed, 'You're wearing a throng? A throng, Kelly?' He literally made me jump out of my skin.

The thing was, my mum had accidentally bought me a pack

Fierce

of thongs instead of sensible knickers. I'd never worn a thong before so I thought I'd give walking around with a piece of string stuck up my arse a go. But my dad wasn't having any of it and he wouldn't let it go. In the hallway of our family home in front of a whole bunch of my best friends, including Sammy and Fleur, he paced up and down saying, 'A throng? No daughter of mine will ever wear a throng – throngs are for whores.'

I was saying to him through my clenched teeth, 'Dad, shut up. You're embarrassing me.' But my dad proceeded to march me down the hallway and into the kitchen, and pinned me to the flowery sofa after grabbing a pair of black scissors from the kitchen drawer. To my utter embarrassment, he cut off my thong in front of my school friends. They were all standing there, huddled around the doorway, in complete silence with their mouths wide open.

This piece of material, no bigger than a string of dental floss, was yanked out of the top of my school jeans and thrown into the air. I died of embarrassment and burst into tears.

My mum, who was no good to me whatsoever, was standing hunched over the kitchen sink laughing her head off while screeching, 'Ozzy! No!'

My friends were in fucking shock. Come to think of it, so was I. I was absolutely hysterical and went from laughing to crying.

My dad was standing there in the family kitchen with my thong (I can't recall what day of the week it represented) in his hand; he tossed it over his shoulder and let it land on the kitchen floor.

That was my first experience of wearing a thong. It was my last for a long time too. It scared me off for life.

Turning Thirteen

'Jack and I *would always go to* the Woolworths on the high street *after we'd left school and* pose for photos *in the tiny booth together.*'

I<small>T</small> wasn't just my father who enjoyed embarrassing me when I was growing up.

My mum would have a good go too. The Saturday after my dad had ripped the thong from my arse, my mum and Aimee had planned a trip to Marks & Spencer.

I was nine and I thought we were going to buy me a new pair of elasticated-waist jeans. They were my favourite style of jeans and I thought I looked so fucking cool when I wore them.

The nearest Marks & Spencer to Welders is in High Wycombe. It's where Mum bought most of our clothes when we were growing up. High Wycombe is a small town twenty-nine miles outside of London but it was the centre of my world when I was growing up. It had all the shops that we loved to spend our five-pounds-a-week pocket money in.

Jack and I would always go to the Woolworths on the High Street after we'd left school and pose for photos in the tiny booth together. Jack would pull faces and I'd cry.

On this particular Saturday, my mum drove me and Aimee and we parked in the

17

town centre. We walked into M&S and that distinct homely smell hit our faces as we stepped out of the cold. I headed straight to the kids' clothes section to check out the new jeans. Then my mum, with Aimee standing next to her, piped up across the shop floor, 'Kelly, just come over here for a second. This lady wants to measure you for something.' It was really busy and everyone looked up when my mum shouted across the shop. I walked over and this woman whipped out this yellow tape measure and wrapped it around my chest over my T-shirt, right in the middle of the shop. Everyone was peering from behind the bras and knickers, looking at me. Mum was standing behind the woman, giggling with Aimee. I realised it was a 'Mum & Aimee' plot. I wasn't in M&S to buy a new pair of jeans at all.

Then the shop assistant announced to the entire shop that my bra size was something ridiculously small like a 28AAA and I'm looking at my mum thinking, 'What the hell are you doing to me?' Mum bought me this flimsy white bra with a flower on it. I really couldn't see the point of it.

Back at home in my bedroom – minus the elasticated jeans – my new bra seemed so complicated to fasten. I wriggled about and finally managed to do it up while standing in my bedroom in front of the mirror. I was praying Jack didn't barge in. I decided I really didn't like wearing a bra. It dug in and was really fucking uncomfortable.

I was the biggest tomboy you could ever meet and a bra just didn't go with my image. It definitely didn't go with Jack's T-shirts with Ghostbusters on the front that I liked to wear. I

Fierce

was mortified about it. Jack and I regularly shared clothes. I lived in jeans, T-shirts and a bright red fleece jacket. I didn't want my little brother Jack to find out about the bra because he really would take the piss. He would probably tell my dad too, which would be even more embarrassing.

I decided to put on my new bra on Monday to keep my mum happy. I felt so bloody self-conscious. It felt like the whole world could see it under my school jumper. As soon as I got to school, I took it off in the toilets and stuffed it in my backpack. None of my friends had a bra. I seemed to grow tits before everyone else. Now I don't seem to have them. How fucking typical.

On the first day I was brave enough to wear it all day, Jack came marching up to me as I stood with all my friends. He proudly pinged the bra strap and stood back pissing himself laughing. Everyone instantly knew that Kelly Osbourne had a bra on. Yeah thanks, Jack.

CHAPTER TWO

BEING AN OSBOURNE

I was always Daddy's Little Girl. I still am.
I can do no wrong in his eyes.

I'T's not like I remember a particular moment when I thought, 'My dad takes drugs.' He just always did. So many years later, having gone through my own experiences with addiction, I can appreciate just how difficult it was for my father as he battled his problems with drink and drugs. I'm so unbelievably proud of him. He is my hero.

When I was eight, I was researching a school project on families. I was going through the boxes of family photographs that my mum kept in her dressing room at Welders. I found one tucked in the corner of the box of my father sitting on an armchair holding up a clear plastic bag with a zip top. It was half-full of white powder.

I ran to find my mum and asked, 'What's this?'

She replied, 'It's flour, darling.' It wasn't until several years later that I actually twigged that my father had been holding a bag of cocaine.

That scenario was quite unusual because my mum has always, always been honest with us. Of course, she didn't sit us down and give us all an in-depth explanation of what drugs were. And I suppose it would have been wholly inappropriate for her to say it was cocaine.

But what she would always do was reassure me, Aimee and Jack that Daddy would be OK. She would say, 'You know your daddy loves you, but he is not very well.' Or she would tell us when he was about to go into rehab, 'Daddy has got to go away for a while.'

She tried her hardest to keep everything in the open, so we didn't think there were secrets that would make us worry.

My dad went into rehab for the first time the day after I was born. I was the only one out of me, Jack and Aimee who was not born at the Wellington Hospital in London. My mum decided not to have an epidural when she had me, so I was born at the Portland.

My dad came to visit me and my mum in the hospital. After he held me for the first time she organised for him to go into rehab. She said that he couldn't come into our lives until he got better. He wasn't in my life for the first three months because he was in rehab somewhere in Palm Springs. It was the Betty Ford Clinic. Later, my mum told me that Dad had walked in there and asked where the wine was. When they said there was no booze, my dad replied, 'Well, I was told that I was coming in here to learn how to drink like a gentleman.' That's what my mum had told him to get him to go.

There would be plenty more rehab visits to come during my

Fierce

life. All of them brought the same hope when Dad came back out. Little did I realise then that my life would be affected too, years later, by addiction and rehab.

My dad's life – his drinking and drug-taking – was just normal to me because I didn't know any different. Only now do I realise how innocent I was about the things that were going on around me. But that's not a bad thing.

My father would always be changing his vice. Rock doctors (these are doctors who like to hang out with bands and give them their drugs) would visit our house all the time. He would smoke cannabis or take 'downers', which are pills that would knock him out. Other times he would become addicted to prescription painkillers.

We'd also go through periods when my dad would be drinking lots because he is a cross-addict, which means he would go from being addicted to drugs to being addicted to alcohol. Actually, when my dad first went back on the booze he would be really good fun. It was like when you go to the pub and have a great night out. Dad would be really happy and loud and up. Life would be great.

But after a while he wouldn't be happy any more. He'd turn into a grumpy drinker. He'd become really angry and I absolutely hated that. He would become unbearable. My mum and dad would have some pretty major fights when my dad was drinking and taking drugs. I knew what my dad had taken pretty much by his behaviour when I walked through the front door after school. If he was being loud and boisterous, he'd usually spent the day drinking.

Being An Osbourne

'My dad's life –

his drinking and drug-taking –

was just normal to me because I didn't

know any different. Only now do I realise

how innocent I was about the things that

were going on around me.

But that's not a bad thing.'

One day when I came home my dad was dressed head to toe in an army uniform. He saluted me as I walked into the kitchen and dumped my bag on the table. What could I say? I think I said, 'Hi, Dad. Been on the booze again?'

If my dad was lying on the sofa with a blanket over him, it meant he had been doing downers all day. He was out of it. Asleep. Nothing was going to bring him round.

There were times when I used to cry. It was so frustrating seeing him like that. And yes, I thought my dad was going to die. When doctors are visiting your house, you worry. Even as a child. It's not easy having an addict in the family. It's really fucking hard. Every time my dad went into rehab I used to think to myself, 'Maybe this time it'll work. I hope this time it works.' I never thought he would fail.

Of course now I know how difficult it can be fighting addictions. If I was mad at him then for taking drugs and drinking, I definitely don't now because I understand. I'm an addict myself.

Once I got really angry with him for behaving the way he did. I think he was addicted to painkillers at the time. It meant he was out of it. He sat me down and said, 'Kelly, are you cold? Are you hungry? Do you want for anything?' Thinking I would finish the sentence with, 'No.' he said, 'Well then.'

But in my head I was thinking, 'I want my dad to be sober.' We were just all so worried about him.

When you are living with an addict, it isn't a 9 a.m. to 5 p.m. thing. It's there all the time. My dad would get really drunk at Christmas and be so miserable. Mum, meanwhile, would

Being An Osbourne

always make a massive fuss in the lead-up to 25 December. Christmas was a big deal in our house. We would have a massive tree in the hallway at Welders. There would be lights in the garden. When we came down in the morning, there would always be a whole stack of presents. My dad was great when we were opening our presents and sometimes would climb into the roof and ring a great big bell. But by lunchtime he'd turn into the Grinch. My dad really hates Christmas. I think it's because it's a time when you're not meant to say shitty things to your family – but my dad would! He'd be grumpy. That wasn't fun. During these times, we pulled together as a family to make sure we had a nice time.

I T'S remarkable how resilient I was when I was growing up. It wasn't as if my dad's drinking and drug-taking dominated my whole life and I had nothing else going on. Even though quite a bit of fucked-up stuff happened, I was actually oblivious to a lot of what Dad was up to. He spent a fair amount of time on the road touring with his band and when he was, our life at home was pretty normal.

When my mum wasn't on the road with my dad, she was there all the time and it was great. But when she went away, either on business or touring with my dad, we were looked after by a whole bunch of nannies. Some were really great, others were shit. I suppose that's the way it goes when you've got a stranger coming into your house. Not even my mum's thorough checks could always stop the freaks from getting through.

I was always Daddy's Little Girl. I still am. I can do no wrong in his eyes. Jack is a mummy's boy.

One time, I was sitting on the edge of the bath with my feet dipped in the water while Mum sat in it. She said to me, 'Kelly, who do you love more? Mummy or Daddy? I thought for a second and replied, 'Daddy, because I don't get to see him much.'

If we went out as a family, I would always be clinging to my dad's side, holding his hand. I'd be wearing my red fleece that I refused to take off ever and my blonde hair would be bobbing on my shoulders.

It's those memories of my childhood that I like to think about. I mean, my father was battling a drink and drug addiction until I was twenty years old. It's nice to have the good memories.

O F course, my parents really fucking love each other. The love between those two has kept our family together throughout the years. It has keept us together through all the drugs, drink, rehab and fights.

Even if my mum and dad had the biggest bust-up ever, if one of them had to leave the house to go away on business or just to the shops, they would always say to each other, 'I love you.'

Mum used to say to me, 'Kelly, you never know what could happen in five minutes.' What she meant was, what if it was the last time they saw each other? Well, that would be just terrible.

I think one of the best things that happened to my dad was Mum deciding to stop drinking. She didn't have a problem with alcohol but when she quit just before she had us, it meant she

UNCLE Tony has always been like my second dad. I love my uncle
Tony so fucking much. He has always, always, always been there
for me.

He's originally from Newcastle. When he was a teenager, he
used to follow my dad around when he was in the band Black
Sabbath. Uncle Tony and his mate would sleep in telephone boxes
because they were so broke but desperate to see Dad perform. One
day my dad, who had spotted Uncle Tony and his mate hanging
around after every gig, said, 'Let me buy you guys breakfast.'
Uncle Tony has been working with my dad ever since. They go
everywhere together. Uncle Tony did everything for us when we
were growing up. Tony used to change my nappies, for fuck's sake.
He is my dad's best friend and they have been together for so long.
I give so much credit to Uncle Tony because he never turned his
back on my dad throughout all the drink and drugs. Believe me,
he's put up with a lot of shit. I'm talking a lot of shit.

He has dedicated his life to my dad. But he wanted to and
he absolutely loves what he does. You should see my uncle Tony
getting ready and preparing before my dad goes on stage. I often
prefer watching my uncle Tony working than my dad because it's
so fucking entertaining and funny. He always wears black: black
long-sleeved top, black trousers, black
tennis shoes. He then ties a fanny pack to his waist with all my
dad's things in it like his inhalers, tea bags for his throat (they're
special tea bags that Uncle Tony puts in hot water so my dad can
sip tea throughout the concert)
and any other stuff Dad needs when he is on stage.

Uncle Tony is so into it. He's running out on to the stage and
running back. At the beginning of every concert, he rubs his
hands and says in a really broad Geordie accent, 'Right, it's on.'

Fierce

Backstage, it's always pitch-black and I'm used to walking around, tripping up over the cables. But no, Tony is there, with the flashlight he's whipped from his fanny pack, pointing it at the floor and guiding me through. And then he's back to the side of the stage, sitting on an upturned bucket. My dad always throws buckets of water out into the audience. He's done it his whole career. And after he's thrown the first one, my uncle Tony will jump up from his upturned bucket, grab the empty bucket my dad's thrown on the stage, fill it up, put it down ready for my dad and return to the side of the stage. He's become an expert in dodging water. He has this sixth sense – he never gets wet. It's all so fucking hilarious. He's my uncle Tony and I love him.

could concentrate on looking after my dad. It would have been disastrous if they'd both been drinking.

In fact, I think they would have killed each other. They'd have ended up like Sid and Nancy. Sid Vicious was in the band the Sex Pistols. He dated the American groupie Nancy Spungen and they lived a very hedonistic life. Nancy was murdered in the late-seventies and Sid was charged with her death before he died of a heroin overdose a few months later. I did not want my parents to end up like them.

I was acutely aware that my father had a reputation for biting the heads off bats. I also knew that he was in a heavy-metal band. He was a musician and he toured a lot. For a long time that's what I thought all dads did.

My mum was determined that we'd have a normal upbringing because she didn't want us to be different from the kids at school. For a start, there was absolutely no swearing in our house. Mum also had a real thing about good table manners. She never wanted us to have table manners like my father's. He's got terrible table manners. He just gobbles it all in and wipes his mouth on the tablecloth.

While my father was behaving the way he was, my mum was busy creating this protective bubble that she kept us all in. She was amazing at giving us security. Don't get me wrong, she couldn't always make us feel protected. We had eyes. We could see what my dad was like at times. But generally, she wanted us to feel loved and stable. I think it's probably quite common for the partner of an addict to feel they have to compensate for some of the upset that is caused within the family.

My mum was always organising great stuff for us to do. When I was nine, I was absolutely obsessed with the American singer Cyndi Lauper. Through my mum's contacts, she was able to take us to meet her. I had never been so fucking excited in the whole of my life. I took my best friend Sammy and my sister

Aimee took her best friend at the time too. I had the biggest smile on my face in the picture that mum took. Bloody hell, I've got the biggest fringe ever though.

Another reason that life didn't feel too stressful with my dad was because I had Jack. He was my best friend when we were growing up. Jack is just over a year younger than me. Aimee is a year older. She used to tell people she was adopted because she had dark hair. She has always  been very close to my mum, especially when we were growing up, and even though there's only a year between us, she is very much the 'older sister'. She was a lot more girly than I was and liked to wear pretty dresses and mess about with dolls and make-up more than I did. She'd always be hanging out with mum in her office or in the lounge. Aimee is really quite shy and has always been an incredibly private person.

People used to think that Jack and I were twins. We both had curly blond hair and you can't tell us apart in many pictures. People are always surprised now when I say I'm a natural blonde. I was such a tomboy I was up for doing all the same things as Jack. During the summer holidays, we'd get up in the morning and put on the same clothes: elasticated jeans, T-shirt, trainers and a fleece.

We would then go into the garden at Welders and you wouldn't see us again until dinner time. I was really boisterous, so we'd climb trees. We played another great game, loosely based around the film *Ghostbusters*. We'd roll around in the mud and chase each other on our bikes. There was absolutely nothing girly about me when I was hanging out with Jack. We did occasionally fight, but never for more than five minutes.

It wasn't until we became teenagers that we began to really fight. The whole way through my childhood, we seriously looked out for each other. To me, my brother is absolutely perfect. I have always struggled with being the older sister because I've never wanted to disappoint him. It's a massive responsibility and I really try hard to be the person that I think he wants me to be.

I also have an older half-brother and sister, Louis and Jessica. They were a big part of our lives when we were growing up – they still are. Dad was married to their mother when he was in Black Sabbath. They were born and brought up in Birmingham with their mum, but they would always come and visit us.

One happy memory I have is us all being in my bedroom one afternoon. We turned the lights off. Jessica and I then made up a dance routine in the dark to one of Take That's songs. Actually, we went through the whole album, we loved them so much. Louis and Jack had torches which they kept shining on to our faces like disco lights.

We all got on really well with Louis and Jessica. Mum wanted so much for us all to get on. She didn't want arguments. Mum tried so hard to please my half-brother and -sister because she didn't want them to feel left out. I understand that, due to the circumstances of how Mum and Dad fell in love, they probably didn't want anything to do with her at the beginning. I never really understood the severity of what happened. If there was ever any resentment on Louis and Jessica's part, then I can see why, because my dad left their mum to be with our mum. But I think as we've all got older, we've made it our business to get along and enjoy seeing each other. I have nieces and nephews – they are the cutest kids. In fact, Jessica's kids now go to the same primary school that I went to when we were living in England.

I REALISED that my family was slightly different when I started school. The penny most definitely started to drop when I saw the other dads who sometimes came to pick up their sons and daughters. They would be standing there in their smart suits. My dad had a different job. He was somewhere in the world performing to an arena of thousands.

I met Sammy on my first day at Gateway School when I was four. It didn't look like a school when I drove up with my mum. It looked more like someone's grand house. It was painted white with two chimneys on the top.

I started to cry as soon as we stepped out of the car. As my mum pulled me along by my hand, I noticed another little girl in the same grey-and-red uniform. She was also crying and standing with her mum. I walked over to her and said, 'Hi. My name is Kelly.' We became best friends for life from that day on. Sammy was the same height as me and we had the same curly blonde hair. Back then, that seemed to be more than enough to become best friends with someone. In the classroom, I sat next to her at a little square table and said, 'You've got the same hair as me. Let's be best friends.'

But there was so much more to mine and Sammy's friendship than our hair. She was the only person who never made fun of me and never questioned anything my parents did. She never said anything. Sometimes the other kids would go, 'There is Ozzy's daughter. He bit the head off a dove.' They must have heard that from their parents. How would they have known that shit? But Sammy would just tell me to ignore them. I loved her for that.

I had this great big, massive fringe. Sammy says to me now, 'Kel, do you remember that great big fringe you had?' And then pisses herself laughing.

I've always been outspoken. During those first few weeks at school, I was constantly getting into trouble because I didn't know what was a grown-up thing to say and what was a child thing to say. In our house we were allowed to talk about whatever we wanted to. If we ever had a question, we would go to my mum and she would tell us. Just like the time when I'd heard girls at school talking about this thing called 'sex'. I thought, I'll speak to Mum and find out what it's all about.

I went to school the next day and told everyone in my class what sex was. I announced to everyone, 'Your dads stick their willies into your mothers' vaginas.' All this sex talk went flying around the school and the teachers were trying to find out who it was who had started it. All hell broke loose.

And then they realised it was me. I was called into the Head's office and he said, 'Kelly, was it you who spread those rumours?'

'One afternoon, *Sammy and I set up the video camera* in her living room and recorded a whole dance routine we'd made up to the Madonna song *"Papa Don't Preach"*.'

I replied, 'I told everyone what sex was.'

I had to sit on a red chair outside the Head's office every day for a week. When I told my mum, she laughed. She knew she hadn't told me anything wrong. I was always free to express myself the way that I wanted to, not the way people thought I should. It was only when I wasn't with my family and at school with the other kids that I realised it wasn't the right way to talk.

Sammy's family was very different to mine. Her mum owned a hair salon and her dad was, and is, the best butcher in Buckinghamshire. Whenever I went to her house for Sunday lunch or breakfast we would have the best sausages. I absolutely loved it.

Sammy's mum used to make us go for a hike every Sunday! She was very organised and always on time. She is a tiny woman and her shoes would always clip-clop on the cobbles. She was forever bollocking my mum for being late to pick me up from school. Sammy would refuse to leave me with the teachers and would insist on waiting, so her mum had to wait too.

I can still remember her parents' home number off the top of my head today – I was always bloody ringing it. I was on the phone to her the whole time. One afternoon, Sammy and I set up the video camera in her living room and recorded a whole dance routine we'd made up to the Madonna song 'Papa Don't Preach'. Sammy was quiet and laid-back.

My other good friend was Fleur Newman. Her dad and mum, Colin and Mette, were my mum and dad's best friends. Colin is also their accountant and business partner. They first met when Colin worked for my mum's dad. I have known Fleur since the day I was born. Mette brought Mum McDonald's while she was in hospital. As they sat eating their chips, Mette laid Fleur next to me in the cot. Fleur knows my life inside out and backwards because of our parents' friendship. She was born to like me. She knows more about how my family works than any of my friends.

Fleur is one of the funniest people I have ever met in my life. She is very set in her ways. You can't mess with Fleur. What I really respect about her is when she says no, she means no. You really can't persuade her. No is no with Fleur. She went to a school in London, but I introduced her to Sammy and we were a great team. She's more like a cousin actually. I can't remember spending a summer or Christmas without her. There are very few people that I trust, but I would tell Fleur anything knowing that she wouldn't tell anyone.

The great thing about Fleur is she sees me as the Kelly who she knew when we were growing up. Around the time that *The Osbournes* started we had come over to London. I'd gone out in Camden, north London, to a bar with Fleur and Sammy. I was stood getting the drinks when this girl came over and said, 'You're Kelly Osbourne and you're fat and ugly. Isn't it a shame you can't be as attractive as your mother?' I thought, 'What the fuck?' So I pushed her and we got into a scuffle. Out of the corner of my eye I saw that her friends had started on Sammy and Fleur and one girl was pulling their hair. I was so pissed off I went marching over and began pushing them off. I felt so bad that they were being attacked because of me.

The story ended up in one of the papers, so Fleur cut it out and framed it. From that day on she has cut out and framed every single embarrassing story and picture of me and hung it on the wall behind her drinks bar at home. That's been one way of keeping my feet on the ground.

When you're in the public eye there are so many fake friends out there. It's so easy to spot them. When I suspect that someone doesn't really want to be my friend but likes the idea of knowing a celebrity, I always ask them to do something for me that I would never ask anyone to do for me. And if they do it and don't turn around and say, 'What the fuck are you asking me to do?' I know that they're a fake. You know, like I'll ask them to pass me my drink even though it's just three inches away from my hand. It's sick that you even have to ask people to do that. But with Sammy it really was very different. She didn't have to be my friend, but she chose to be.

During school time, my life was pretty much the same as everyone else's in my class. When my dad was home from touring, I was sometimes very reluctant to bring my friends home after school. I wasn't always sure what state my dad would be in and I didn't want to be embarrassed.

When we broke up for the summer holidays, I knew that I would be going off to do something completely different from my friends. My mum didn't like us spending too much time away from Dad so, whenever we could, we would always go and join him on the road. It meant we got to fly all over the world to places like America, Japan and Europe. We were bloody lucky.

We would stay with my mum and dad on the tour bus. We had our own little beds and we'd drive from city to city. It was fantastic fun. I sent Sammy and Fleur postcards from all the different places that we used to visit.

When we were with my father on tour he would take us on to the stage during one of his songs and the crowd would go absolutely mental. He would be holding Jack in his arms and I would be holding on to one of his legs and Aimee would be clutching the other. Mum would be smiling proudly from the side of the stage.

On a couple of the tours, the heavy-metal band Mötley Crüe would be supporting my dad. When my dad was due on stage, everyone who was with us went to be with him. So the guys from Mötley Crüe would come and babysit us on the tour bus. I suppose they weren't your conventional babysitters. But they were bloody cool.

I was lucky because I had Fleur with me on some of those trips, but being away from your friends during the school holidays is always a bit weird. Going back to school after those trips was always a bit strange for me. I'd had such a different summer holiday to all my other friends. I'd tell them what I'd been up to and my good friends thought it was cool. I'm sure some felt a little jealous, but at that age they didn't show it too much. When you're a kid you just want to be like all your friends. So even being picked out as being Ozzy Osbourne's daughter was a big fucking deal. No one else in my class was Ozzy Osbourne's daughter. But it was when I got older that the more hurtful bullying started.

CHAPTER THREE

I LOVE A GOOD SCHOOL PROJECT

I was so desperate to fit in that I would say I was going to be a nursery-school teacher when I was older.

W HEN I was nine I was diagnosed with dyslexia. Before then, I think my teachers genuinely thought I was stupid. I'm sure of it. They would give me the most ridiculous exercises to do. I was given a page full of drawings and I'd have to label them. I knew what a cat and dog was for fuck's sake. That isn't what dyslexia is about. It was so humiliating to be given that sort of work to do.

It was my mum who picked up my dyslexia. My dad is dyslexic too. She realised I had it too when she read my school reports and cottoned on. The teachers said my spelling wasn't improving like it should be. My mum was really insulted when they wrote those things. She didn't want people to think that I was stupid. She didn't want me to think that for that matter either.

One night Mum sat me down in the lounge at Welders and told

me all about what dyslexia was. Because of my dad having it, she knew exactly how to deal with it. She reassured me and told me I had nothing to worry about. It made me feel a whole lot better.

It wasn't until we moved to America when I was thirteen that my dyslexia was tackled properly at a school that specialised in teaching kids with the condition. I've put a lot of the stuff they taught me then into practice now. Dyslexia affects the way the brain processes words and letters, making it difficult for sufferers to read, spell and write. About four per cent of people in Britain have it.

I realised there was something keeping me apart from the rest of the class because I had started to hate reading out loud during lessons. It was something that began to worry me. In the morning, when I was getting ready for school I'd sometimes think, 'Oh my God, everyone is going to make fun of me if I read out loud today. They'll laugh if I get a word wrong.' In the end I refused to read to the class.

I knew how to read, but in my head. It was when I had to read aloud that I'd get all the words confused. For example, if the sentence said: 'It rained today.' I would read it out as: 'Rained today it.' My brain process would jumble up the words. I do it with numbers as well.

My spelling also suffered because of the dyslexia. I used to spell phonetically. So if someone said the name 'Siobhan' I would spell it 'Shivorn'.

My mum bought me a computer so I could do my homework and then spell-check it all. It really helped and improved my spelling.

Around the same time, my mum noticed that Jack was struggling too. He was also diagnosed with dyslexia. It's obviously something that runs in the family.

Over the years, I've found ways of dealing with my dyslexia, but it has been a massive struggle for me. It's something I have to work on every day. Technology – like predictive text on my mobile phone – has made it easier.

When I decided I wanted to do this book, I did ask someone to help me. I knew exactly what I wanted to say, but I realised that chatting to someone who would type what I'd said would be far more practical.

In my line of work, I have to make sure I'm really focused. My peers will walk in, read the autocue and go home. But I have to be prepared if I am going to present a TV show. I have to write down what I'm going to say and memorise it.

Years later, when I got a job at Radio 1 co-hosting *The Surgery* on a Sunday night, I would get so nervous when it came to the script read-through before the evening show. Sometimes I wouldn't be able to read out loud and I'd fuck it up.

In the end, I confessed to my producer that I was severely dyslexic. I explained that the way I had learned to deal with it was to prepare. So I explained that they wouldn't be able to just shove something under my nose with a second's notice. Of course, I knew it was live radio and I would have to react to people phoning and emailing in to the show. The one thing I have learned is that when you're dyslexic it's amazing how clever you become. You become very canny at covering things up.

I Love A Good School Project

WHEN I was twelve, I started at Pipers Corner School. It was a private school tucked away in a corner of the Buckinghamshire countryside near High Wycombe. It's a boarding school and a day school, and I came home every day. Usually Mum or the nanny would come and pick me up. We had to wear a white shirt, red jumper and grey skirt. It was really posh and incredibly strict.

From day one I made sure I talked to absolutely everyone and I made lots of friends.

I could have gone to the Italia Conti Academy of Theatre Arts in London. My sister Aimee went there for a while and my mum had gone there when she was little. It was a performing-arts school for kids. I didn't want to go. Fuck, no. I didn't want to go to do ballet or whatever. I appreciate the ballet. I think it's beautiful and I can understand why someone would want to be a dancer. But fuck, not me.

Instead, during those first few weeks at Pipers Corner School, I was so conscious of the fact that I came from a family with a famous dad that I would lie about what I wanted to be when I was older. I was so desperate to fit in that I would say I was going to be a nursery-school teacher. Also, I thought that if I said I wanted to be a rock star like my dad they would laugh in my face. But I had sort of planned in my head that I would become a businesswoman because that's what my mum was. I'd watched her at her desk doing all her filing and paperwork and I wanted to do the same sort of thing. Despite the dyslexia, I loved a good school project. I couldn't get enough of them. I was meticulous with how I planned them. You name it, I bet

I did a bloody project on it. Eggs, chairs, Indian spices . . . I once spent hours patiently sticking tiny grains of spice into my exercise book. My parents never helped me with my projects. No. Never. Although Mum was very encouraging when we were at school. She would buy all the arts and craft things and made sure we had everything we needed, but we would do the work ourselves. I absolutely loved covering my books in crisp and sweet wrappers. And tinfoil . . . what the hell! When was the last time you ever heard of anyone doing that?

I used to buy *TVHits* magazine because you got free stickers. I would cover my folders with pictures of Ant & Dec, Boyzone, the Spice Girls and NSYNC. Much to my father's dismay, I really fucking love pop music.

Science and history were my best subjects because they're fact, fact, fact. You can't change fact, can you? Either it is or it isn't. Of course people can change history. But the facts always remain the same.

You can forget maths. It made no bloody sense to me at all. It was the dyslexia. I would get all the numbers the wrong way round. On my report card one year it said: 'Maths is not Kelly's favourite subject. But when she concentrates, she does very well.'

I had no problem with making my voice heard. On one report card, the teacher put under oral communication: 'Kelly has excellent communication skills.' No shit! Blame my parents. Years of being on tour with my father meant I could talk to anyone of any age.

When I was at school I mothered everyone. Fuck knows why. I was very good at sorting everyone out and being Miss Practical.

I Love A Good School Project

We had a school newspaper and I was the agony aunt. My classmates would write in with their problems about homework or bullying or whatever. I would print one of the letters with my answer. I loved it. I think I get my need to mother from my own mother. She's very good at just getting on with things and being practical.

I am not joking when I say that I have absolutely everything from my school days. There's a massive trunk outside my bedroom at Welders in the UK crammed full of all my exercise books, reports, projects, letters . . . That's Mum for you. She's a bloody hoarder.

Dad was always banned from parents' evenings at Pipers Corner School. On the few previous occasions he had turned up, he would fall asleep as the teachers spoke to him and Mum.

Another time, as the teacher sat behind the desk talking to my parents, my dad kept pulling up his T-shirt and showing her his stomach. I mean, for fuck's sake. My dad does this crazy thing where, after he has eaten something, he lifts up his T-shirt to see if he's gained any weight. That's why he was doing it.

I think my mum banned him, not the school. They probably thought he was funny. Everyone else bloody did. In the end, my mum used to go by herself. I wasn't bothered that my dad didn't go to parents' evenings. It meant that everyone wouldn't be talking about it at school the next day. 'Did you hear what Kelly's dad did last night?' All that sort of shit.

My dad hated school and I felt the same when I hit my teens and moved to America. I'm incredibly proud of my dad and what he's achieved on his own merits without an education. Of

Fierce

course, getting an education is vitally important. But I think I realised at an early age that I would be one of those people who learned outside the classroom. I would get a different type of education.

It was blatantly obvious that I had a good grasp of what drugs were. I was blatantly way more knowledgeable on the subject than my innocent school friends.

Once, in English, we had to write about the dream we'd had the night before. Thinking about it, what if you'd not had a dream the night before? The teacher didn't consider that. And you can't always remember them, can you? I wrote the following (I'm writing about a dream within a dream):

'My Dream'

When I went to bed that night I was thinking about those girls, you know the ones who smoke and take drugs.

The cool gang that's what they call themselves. The high forces.

I wonder what it would be like to be in a gang.

I fell asleep and found myself smoking. It tasted disgusted, but I thought it was cool and then I sniffed something that made me feel dizzy.

I feel dizzy and I fall to the floor. They all said: 'She has had an overdose.' She's in bed. Put her in the dumpster.

I Love A Good School Project

I then I woke up all sweaty and realised I was just dreaming. And thank god. I am not hanging around them again.

Where the fuck did I get that shit from? Now I can't even remember writing it. I'm actually shocked. I was twelve years old. It must have come from knowing about my dad. It was obviously something that was on my mind.

Similarly, when I read the book *Junk* for the first time, I knew what everything meant. No one else at my school had a clue. *Junk* was written by the author Melvin Burgess. The main characters, Tar and Gemma, get together and then leave home. They end up living with some squatters. In the second half of the book they become heroin addicts. It's quite detailed in its explanation of what drugs can do. When I say I was knowledgeable on drugs, of course I was aware of the names of different drugs, but I didn't know the details of how they were taken. *Junk* was there with all the details and it also made me realise that drugs affected lots of other people apart from just my family. When the book came out in 1996 it was quite controversial because even though it was aimed at young adults, many parents thought it was unsuitable for their teenagers.

Everyone was talking about it at school and I wanted to find out what it was all about for myself. One night after school, I went to WHSmith in Beaconsfield, which is a town near Welders. I saw it on the shelf. Firstly, I was attracted to the bright-green cover with a needle on the front. But of course I'd heard what it was about, so I wanted to read it and know what was going

Fierce

on. As I flicked through the pages, I really related to the story and could understand what the characters were going through. I'm pleased I read *Junk*. It gave me a greater understanding of drugs and it actually explained a lot of things to me. I would recommend this book to anyone. When I'm reading in my head, I don't struggle to read as much as if I have to read out loud. Also, I found it easier to educate myself – I learned loads more that way than sitting in a classroom being force-fed facts!

I think it's so stupid of parents not to talk to their kids and inform them about drugs. I was given every reason not to become a drug addict. But this is the interesting bit: if it hadn't been for my family being so open about drugs then I think I would have been dead by the time I was twenty because they wouldn't have known how to help me. My mum has always known what to do and where to go when she's suspected I've needed help. What if she hadn't?

OBVIOUSLY, when we got to school age, it meant we couldn't go on tour with dad any more. That was saved for the school holidays and, if he was only in Europe, weekends.

I used to absolutely hate it when my parents went on tour. We all did. I used to try every trick in the book to get them to stay. In my bedroom in Welders, surrounded by my fairyland mural, I'd stand on my bed and piss all over the duvet and sheets. That would mean I had to go and sleep in Mum and Dad's bed. I did that from the age of five until I was thirteen. When I was in bed with my mum and dad, I knew they weren't going away on tour – or rather, I thought they couldn't go away on tour. I just hated it so much when I was apart from them. Of course, we had some really great nannies at times like Kim, who came from Newcastle. She was lovely. And when she got married I was a bridesmaid with Aimee and Jack was the pageboy. But as lovely as some of the nannies were, I would have preferred it if Mum and Dad had stayed at home.

Every time they went away, I would write letters begging them: 'Please don't leave me.'

My mum's kept all of them. They're at Welders in one of the trunks on the landing outside our bedrooms. My mum keeps everything, although she doesn't keep anything that isn't attached to a memory. But most things are. I think it's something you can only fully understand if you're a mother yourself. At Welders, she has one room that's just dedicated to photographs. She has cupboards and cupboards full of them. She also has an island in the middle of the room with a glass top. Underneath she has laid out all her favourite photographs so when she goes in she can see them all.

I don't keep everything, but I have trouble throwing things away because I'm worried I'm going to want it later in life. When you're dead you can't take anything with you, but while I'm still living I like to know where I've been and keep the things that have meant something to me.

It's absolutely heartbreaking to read over the letters that I sent Mum before she went away. There's one that says – and I must have been naughty because I'm apologising for something too –

Fierce

'To Mummy. I am sorry. Please forgive me. I love you very much. You do not know how much I love you. Please don't go to Japan. I will miss you too much. Love from Kelly.'

I'd scribble them while sitting on my bed in my bedroom. Then I would run out and down the spiral staircase that led to my parents' bedroom. I would tip-toe to their door, fold up the piece of paper and push it through the gap at the bottom so they would find it when they came to open the door.

In the days leading up to my parents' trips abroad, I would spend hours sitting on that spiral staircase sobbing, 'Don't go. Please don't go, Mummy and Dadda.' (I always refer to my father as Dadda. I still do today.)

WHEN my father used to go away on his own, we had a rotation list for my mum's bed. This is how it went: my mum would sleep on the right-hand side, one of us would be in the middle, one on the left and another would lie at the bottom. Actually, it was only me and Jack who swapped, Aimee would always be next to Mum.

On some trips, Mum and Dad would have to leave really early in the morning. They didn't like to wake us because it was too early. Also, it would have made us even more upset. So Mum devised this little way of letting us know how much we were loved and that she was thinking about us too. It must have been really hard for her to leave behind her babies. Mum would go around the house and write on everything in one of her red

I Love A Good School Project

'*In the days leading up to my parents' trips abroad, I would spend hours sitting on that spiral staircase sobbing,* **"Don't go. Please don't go,** *Mummy and Dadda."*'

lipsticks. I would lift up the toilet seat in the bathroom and there would be a message written underneath the lid saying: 'I love you, Kelly.' Or she would write on the wall behind my bed: 'Love you. Love, Mummy.'

They would be all over the place: on the walls, on the fridge door, in the bathroom. She still does it today. It's her thing. Jack still has one of those messages. She wrote it when we were living in Welders. It's in red lipstick on the wall above his bed.

As soon as I woke up on the morning Mum and Dad had left the house, I would race down to their bedroom. I'd hunt around for one of Mum's nighties and I would scrunch it to my face and breathe in her perfume. I loved the fact it reminded me of my mum and it was a tremendous comfort. I would sleep with it under my pillow until the day they returned and then I would put it back in her drawer until next time.

During the time they were away, my life would be ruled by the stupid tour books that every band's management company has made up. They basically have the dates for each venue followed by the names and numbers of all the hotels Mum and Dad would be staying at in each city. Then there would be a page of names and numbers of every single person involved in the tour. I would go to my mum's office and find the tour book and keep it opened on the calendar page. After my dad had performed at each venue, I'd do a bright red tick across it and count down the days.

When Mum went on tour with my dad she was incredibly torn at times. There had been a period when I was about six that we moved to America for a few months and had actually gone to school there. It had been so my mum could keep us all together. We soon moved back to the UK. But moving out there permanently was obviously something that my mum was thinking about.

In 1996, my mum came up with an idea for a festival called Ozzfest. It was a massive tour around America of heavy metal and hard rock bands. Some of them were already established and others were up and coming. It was really successful and Dad was the headline act with his band. Because it was an American festival, it meant my mum had to go there more often for meetings and to set things up.

In the summer after I'd turned thirteen there was a school trip to Wales. Aimee had also joined the school at this point. In the past, we had not always been able to go on the school trips because we would sometimes be away with Dad. But we wanted to be with our friends, so we signed up for the three-day visit.

When we got to the hostel, we soon realised that the food was going to be shit. Aimee and I are really fussy eaters. We don't like fancy food. On the menu it was all kidney and haggis and pretty crazy shit. Well, it was to us. It wasn't that I was so much bothered about the taste. I just didn't like the idea of eating some poor fucking animal's kidneys.

Aimee and I hardly ate a thing for three fucking days and we were absolutely starving. The packed lunch that my mum had done for us both to eat on the way, we'd made last during the trip. We'd rationed it to keep us going. On the coach on the way back our stomachs were rumbling. When we stopped at a service station on the motorway, I turned to Aimee who was sitting in the seat behind me and said, 'Aimee, let's get as much food as we can.' The problem was, I only had a few pennies left because we'd only been allowed to take five pounds and I'd spent it on souvenirs and shit.

In the shop, I bought a packet of cheese and onion crisps. But I was so fucking hungry that I'd eaten them before I'd even got back to the coach. I was sitting in my seat next to the window and as the coach pulled away I poked my head between the two seats and whispered to Aimee behind me: 'Aimee, I'm starving. Have you got any food left? Can I have some?'

It was just at a moment when the coach was the quietest it had been on the trip that my sister replied, 'Kelly, your breath fucking stinks. Fuck off.'

Cartoon-style, the coach weaved to the side of the road that led to the motorway and practically screeched to a halt. One of the teachers came marching down the aisle and said, 'Kelly, who swore at you just then?'

I just kept looking forward and said, 'I don't know, Miss.'

As if I was going to dob my sister in it. As much as we didn't get on at times, sibling rivalry and all that, there was no way I was going to dob on my sister. There was absolutely no fucking way.

The teacher knew it was Aimee, but she was trying to get me to admit it. When we got back to school, Aimee and I both got suspended and a letter went home to our parents. My mum was in the kitchen and read the letter that was summoning her to see the Head. In our bedrooms, Aimee and I were bracing

I Love A Good School Project

ourselves for the biggest telling off we'd ever had from Mum – and the school.

I said to Aimee, 'This is it. We've had enough warnings. Mum is going to lose it. She hates swearing and she is going to go absolutely nuts.'

I'd already said to Aimee just before we went in the Head's office, 'We're done for, Aimee. Kiss your sweet ass goodbye.'

I mean, we're talking about a school where you'd get a bloody detention if you used the wrong coloured pen, so you can imagine why they didn't take too kindly to Aimee saying 'Fuck off'.

Sitting in the Head's room with the teacher and my mum, I was perched on a plastic chair with my hands clenched underneath at either side waiting for the Head to say that we were going to get expelled.

Mum said to the teacher, 'OK. Explain to me what happened."

The Head came out with all this stuff about how Aimee had sworn at me on the school trip. But I had refused to say it was her when asked about it.

Mum just replied, 'Do you really expect sisters to tell on each other?' She continued, 'All she said at the end of the day was: "Fuck off". What is so wrong with that? Why didn't you just give her a detention?'

Aimee and I looked up and were smiling at each other. We couldn't believe that Mum was taking our side.

Mum then just stood up and said, 'You know your problem? You need to get fucked.' Then she turned to me and Aimee and said: 'Come on we're going.'

We couldn't believe what had just happened. We were absolutely pissing ourselves laughing.

As we walked across the car park to where Mum had parked she said to us, 'That's it. We're going to America to be with your dad.'

I Love A Good School Project

CHAPTER FOUR

BECOMING AMERICANISED

I'd pretty much come to the conclusion quite early on that Beverly Hills was not real life.

AFTER being brought up in rural Buckinghamshire where the most exciting place to hang out was Pizza Hut, I couldn't believe my luck when we moved to Los Angeles in the summer of 1998.

We'd spent periods of times there during the holidays when we were kids, but this time was different because I was thirteen and could really appreciate the massive shopping malls and movie theatres that were all just five minutes away. Everything was local and twenty-four hours and quick, quick, quick! You want a pizza at 3 a.m.? No fucking problem.

Our move to America made sense. In the UK it had got to the stage where we were spending too much time apart from my dad because he was always touring or recording in America. My mum was spending more and more time away from us too. As my father's manager, she was always being called back on tour because Dad was being so naughty and had fallen off the tracks again. He would be off the rails on drink and drugs.

My mum would get phone calls from the crew who were with him on tour in America, saying, 'Sharon, you've got to come back, Ozzy is off his head.'

There was no master plan when we moved to America. We literally packed our bags, left Welders and jumped on a plane for the eleven-hour flight to Los Angeles. I was too excited to give a shit about whether I would fit in or make friends. It was going to be fun to hang out in Los Angeles for a while. That's the great thing about growing up with a dad who is on the road touring. You do become very used to change. But I was really missing my best friends Sammy and Fleur.

Every time my mum was on the phone to her business partner Colin Newman, who is Fleur's dad, I'd screech in the background, 'Put Fleur on. I want to speak to Fleur.' I was excited about making friends at my new school. But that whole being the new girl thing was going to be absolutely shit. I started writing to Sammy and Fleur. We made a pact that they would come and visit during the next school holidays, which I was really looking forward to. I planned to take them swimming and shopping.

MY mum registered me at a school about ten minutes' drive away from the Beverly Hills Hotel, which everyone calls

Fierce

the Pink Palace. We were staying there while we looked for a new house.

I thought, 'Fuck me. This is a cool place to live.'

The Pink Palace is on Sunset Boulevard in Beverly Hills, which is an area in Los Angeles. The Palace is the most exclusive hotel in the city and has kept its traditions from the 1950s. It's very old-school Hollywood. It's impossible to go there and not see an A-list star. It really values its guests' privacy, which is why it's so popular. My mum has been going to there since the 1970s and all the staff really look after her. It has the most amazing spa, where my mum used to get all her treatments done.

We were staying in one of the twenty-one private bungalows that sit in the hotel's tropical gardens. The bungalow had a swimming pool and a Jacuzzi and the sun was always shining.

Every celebrity you can think of dines or has meetings at the Beverly Hills Hotel. It was such a surreal experience for me. On my first day of school, as I walked through the lobby, Tom Hanks was having breakfast in the Polo Lounge, which is the hotel's famous restaurant. I was lucky if I passed a sheep on my way to school in the UK, it was so remote.

From that day on, I saw every actor, TV presenter and singer in that place. Was it cool? Hell, yeah. There was Johnny Depp, Tom Cruise, Matt Damon, Julia Roberts – everyone! My new school, Hawthorne School, was so fucking different to Pipers Corner School, the all-girls school that I'd left behind in the UK. I'd been used to going to a school where there were just 580 pupils. Hawthorne had more than 5,000 pupils and it was mixed. I felt my new school was not going to be anywhere near

Becoming Americanised

as strict as the one I'd left behind, which wasn't going to be a bad thing. I didn't have to wear a uniform at my new school either, which meant I had been shitting myself because I didn't know what to wear.

Kelly Osbourne
Westmark Lions

I'd just arrived in America, so I wasn't up on what everyone else would be wearing. At my last school, I'd worn a bloody cape! So Mum took me to Fred Segal, which is a really popular store in America. It instantly became my favourite place. It was Mum's favourite store too and it certainly beat the Marks & Spencer shopping trips. No offence. Because Fred Segal is one of the coolest places to hang out in LA, it's always full of people desperate to get noticed. There's always a bunch of wannabe actors or models just hanging out, hoping a model scout or acting agent will pick them out. They're all fighting for the same acting job or modelling assignment, so will do whatever it takes to get seen. The plus side is that it's full of totally different clothes and accessories. I've never gone there and not found something I've liked. They've got really cool clothes and that's the reason it's been around since the seventies.

M Y mum took me to school on my first day. The place was massive. There was a stream of people going through the gates. It was like going to one of my dad's concerts at a big arena. I was taken to the principal's office and handed a

Fierce

timetable. That was it. I was very much the British girl and my accent really made me stand out and soon enough I fell into that whole transatlantic accent thing. I'd go up at the end of sentences and all that shit. But, after a while, I realised I wanted to keep my English accent.

I hated Hawthorne. I hated that school. I got lost in the crowd. It was a big school, so sometimes I would literally get bloody lost in the crowd. But it was more about the American education system which is just so different to the UK one. I didn't have a clue what was going on in the lessons. Because I had dyslexia it meant that I was doubly struggling. It didn't really seem to be working out for me at the new school.

It was around this time that I was also diagnosed with ADHD (Attention Deficit Hyperactivity Disorder). There are different levels and symptoms, but generally it means that a person finds it difficult to maintain attention without being distracted. Jack was diagnosed with it at the same time too. I think that having ADHD was another reason I was struggling to understand the new lessons. As a child I was always bouncing about and jumping around, so I probably had it from as far back as then. My parents probably thought I was just being a lively kid.

I am someone who is always on the go. When I was sitting in the back of a classroom, not understanding half the things that were going on and something grabbed my attention outside, I would just lose concentration. That would probably have happened even if I'd not had ADHD, I was so far behind in the lessons.

I think it was my mum who first thought I might have ADHD. She took me to see the doctor in LA. He prescribed the drug Adderall, which is given to patients with ADHD to improve their concentration. It has amazing results.

After a couple of weeks, you could really see the difference. My school work was one hundred times better. But the downside was that it practically turned me into a robot. Mum would say to me, 'Kelly, have you done your homework?'

I would reply back to her in a monotone voice, 'Yes, Mum. I have done my homework.' The drug was turning me into a zombie. I was losing my personality.

Yes, it did make me focused and I was doing much better at school. But I didn't like the person I had become. My mum didn't like who I turned into either, so she took me off the drug.

IN Los Angeles, I discovered that the kids were far more tuned into 'celebrity' life. Back in the UK, my friends really didn't give a shit that my father was Ozzy Osbourne because at that time he was bigger in America. I think I'd underestimated what effect it would have on my life or how people would react to me at school.

Once it got out that my dad was Ozzy Osbourne, I never really stood a chance with the bullies. I was a great target for them. The bullying was mainly name-calling. But only someone who has experienced it knows how hurtful being

Fierce

called names can be. It really affects your whole world. Whoever said that dumb rhyme? 'Sticks and stones will break your bones, but names will never hurt you.' They were talking absolute bullshit.

This group of lads would shout down the school corridors after me when I walked with my friends. They'd say, 'Kelly, your dad's a drug addict.' I would think, 'God, you're original. Tell me something I don't know.'

I would shout back, 'You're so fucking funny.'

In America, my dad was in the papers all the time for various reasons. It was a case of: 'Ozzy strikes again . . .' And so does the bullying at school for his daughter, Kelly. I'm not going to lie, it was absolutely shit. It was mainly the guys who would take the piss. They'd also sing songs like, 'Kelly is smelly, she has a big belly and her dad is on the telly.' There was one afternoon when I went back to the hotel and cried to my mum. Between sobs I said, 'Of all the names. Why did you have to call me Kelly? Because I do have a belly, Mum?'

My mum hugged me and said: 'My darling, you're gorgeous. Don't listen to them.'

I LEFT Hawthorne School – thank God. I'd hardly been there because I kept suffering from tonsillitis and was off sick quite a bit. I was happy to leave. I hated it. I moved to another school called Westmark, which specialised in teaching kids with dyslexia. It was great. Aimee joined too.

On my first day, I met Molly and Tali, who instantly became my best friends. I walked into the classroom and I was immediately drawn to Molly, who had different colour bracelets going all the way up her arm. Tali was sitting next to her, laughing. They were the only two who seemed like fun. With the greatest of respect to them, we were known at school as the Three Fat Girls! I'm not joking. Some of the kids at school knew about my dad. Molly and Tali were not bothered and that's why I wanted to be their friend. I'm still in touch with them now. Molly is a stylist to the stars. Tali works in communications in Israel.

I became very Americanised thanks to those two. After school, everyone used to hang out at the nearest shopping mall and they took me with them. Our favourite was Century City, which is one of the biggest in Los Angeles. It was here that I did a lot of my growing up. The deal was we'd all go home straight after school and do our homework for an hour. Then my mum would drop me off outside where the valets would

stand. That was another great thing about LA. Whenever you drive to a shopping mall or hotel, there is always someone waiting to meet you. They take your keys and park your car for you. It saves so much time not having to piss around looking for a parking space. That was the spot where my mum

always used to drop me off. I would call her when I wanted picking up. If I was making my own way home, I had to be back by 10 p.m. at the latest.

Fierce

I'd run from the car and walk over this bridge that used to join Century City to a little field where we'd all hang out. The sun would still be hot at 5 p.m. and we'd all lie out and talk. It would usually be the girls in one corner and the guys in another. We used to keep running back to the shopping centre to grab a drink at Coffee Bean, which sells hot drinks, cold drinks, smoothies and cakes. In Los Angeles there are Coffee Beans on every bloody street corner. In the UK, they have pubs.

Some of the kids in my class that I used to hang out with had started smoking. And sure, I was interested in giving it a go because all my friends were trying it. I'd grown up with a father who was a smoker. There was one guy who was puffing away on a Marlboro Red thinking he looked really cool. Apart from that type of cigarette being really fucking strong, it also proved he didn't knowwhat he was doing because they were the most advertised brand ever. I took a lit cigarette from between his fingers as we lay on the grass and took a drag.

I started coughing and spluttering straight away and had to hand it back quickly. I didn't like the taste. I definitely didn't like the smell. I thought, 'Well, Kelly, you're not going to be a smoker.'

I'd pretty much come to the conclusion quite early on that Beverly Hills was not real life. Well, not to me, anyway. There are great things to do there and the sun is always shining. But LA is a fantasy life. The streets are lined with massive mansions all sitting amongst immaculate gardens with a bunch of fancy cars in the driveway. It's all about: 'Look how much money I have. Look at how successful I am.'

I mean, how can it be real when the local shops are Gucci and Prada? That's not life. Where's the Tesco? Where's the corner shop? I saw it for what it was in those early days and tried to concentrate on the fun stuff.

THE first summer we spent in LA was an absolute blast. I mean look, we got in the car, drove for five minutes and we were at Rodeo Drive; the shopping street Julia Roberts made more famous in *Pretty Woman*. There's every designer shop you can think of from Mulberry to Ralph Lauren. I used to love visiting that street and laughing at all the women with stretched, plastic-surgery-enhanced faces – I call them Vegas Face. It means they've had bad plastic surgery. There'd be whole bunch of them struggling with their millions of bags courtesy of their husbands' credit cards.

There were fun places for teenagers to go to. My mum would always take me for a cheeseburger at Carney's Express, which was a diner on a disused train sitting at the edge of Sunset Boulevard, the street that runs through Los Angeles and Beverly Hills.

People would carry dogs under their arms with little designer outfits on with matching collars. I couldn't believe they had shops that actually specialised in doggy clothes. I'd never seen anything like it. My mum used to take us to the Beverly Center, which is a massive shopping mall on about eight different levels on the edge of West Hollywood and Beverly Hills. I'd never been to such a huge place. Inside were Macy's and Bloomingdale's, which are well-known department

68

' "*Now, Jack!*

Now, Jack."

Jack would whip out his gun

and squirt some

innocent woman

'

out shopping.

stores in America. There were shops that I'd never heard of like Banana Republic, which sounded like a political fruit.

The sun was always shining in LA so my mum bought a convertible car. Uncle Tony would drive us everywhere. My dad can't drive. Well, he can, but he hasn't passed his test. He always used to drive around Welders when we lived there.

When we first moved to LA it was all fun, fun, fun times. Uncle Tony would drive me, Jack and Dad along Sunset Boulevard. Dad and I used to sit in the back and Jack would be in the front. My dad would chuck stink bombs through the doors of the shops. They'd roll in and land at the feet of the women buying their designer clothes. They'd look down and pull the funniest faces or run out. We'd be sitting in the car pissing ourselves laughing. Or Jack would have a squirt gun hidden by his feet. My dad would be looking for people to squirt and then he'd shout: 'Now, Jack! Now, Jack.' Jack would whip out his gun and squirt some innocent woman out shopping.

Living in LA was cool. But some crazy shit was also starting to happen too, which is just typical of my family. One day Jack, Mum, Aimee and I were eating at a deli in Beverly Hills. This man started calling my mum a 'nigger fucker'. He was standing about a couple of yards away from us in the LA sunshine screaming, 'You're a nigger fucker.' Everyone was stopping and watching us. It was really embarrassing.

Aimee turned to Mum and said, 'Why is Tony Curtis calling you a nigger fucker, Mum?' The man in question really looked like the Hollywood actor Tony Curtis, who was a friend of Mum's.

I was too busy thinking, 'Oh my God. That is the most disgusting thing I have ever heard anyone say. How can they say that? How can they use the N word?'

My mum just grabbed us all and hurried us along into a shop. When we got back to the hotel Mum was forced to admit that it was her father, Don Arden, who had been calling her those nasty words.

We had a grandfather. Mum had always told us that our grandparents were dead. Whenever I would ask her what they were like or what they did, she would just brush it off and change the subject. Most of the time she said they weren't alive any more. We believed her. Why wouldn't we? It's so strange how unaffected I was and still am about my mum's father. Jack and I really didn't care. It didn't mean anything to us. The most shocking thing to me and Jack was the language that had come out of his mouth.

Back at the hotel, my mum asked us if we wanted to meet our grandfather. I thought, I've not had him in my life for fourteen years, I don't know a lot about him apart from the bad stuff, and I know that there must have been a very good reason for my mum to want to keep him away from us. So I thought, I'll leave it at that.

I did meet him once. He came over for food at our house. I never called him 'Grandad'. I hardly spoke to him. I didn't give a shit – he was just some old man.

Years later, Mum made her peace and paid for him to be put into a care home in LA after he became too ill to look after himself.

When he died in 2008 I didn't feel anything except confusion, because I didn't expect my mum to be so upset. It hit her hard. I think it made her realise that it's not always worth shutting people out of your life for so long over arguments in the past.

I WAS fourteen and I'd not started my period. I wasn't bothered. I didn't care. I didn't want to get my period. I just didn't want to have blood coming out of my vagina once a month. By this point we'd moved out of the Beverly Hills Hotel and into 906 North Beverly Drive.

It was a detached house behind big black gates with a balcony at the front. I wouldn't say it was one of those massive, massive houses, but it was cool. It wasn't far from school and all the places we liked to hang out.

One night, at around 9 p.m. I was sitting in my bedroom when I started to get the most God-awful stomach ache.

I walked across the hallway from my bedroom and into my parents' room to tell my mum. She was sitting on the edge of her bed and she said, 'Kelly, you're just making it up because you don't want to go to school tomorrow.'

I was pleading, 'No, Mum. My stomach really does hurt.'

But she replied in her deep I'm-not-taking-any-shit voice, 'Kelly, go to bed. If you don't go to bed, that's it!'

I was like, 'All right. Calm down. Whatever.'

I woke up the next morning and went for my morning wee in the en suite bathroom. I'm not joking, I looked down into my knickers and thought I had shat myself in my sleep. I went running into Mum's room crying and screaming. She told me to calm down and said she would come with me to the toilet to try and sort it out. She took one look and said, 'No, you idiot, you've got your period. You're a woman now.'

I looked at her, sat on the floor, and started crying again. I couldn't stop. I thought, 'So what to being a woman if this is what happens.'

I stood up, grabbed my mum's hands and said, 'Don't you dare tell anyone. You must not tell anyone. Promise me you won't tell?' My mum showed me what I had to do with the sanitary towels and I stood there next to her in the bathroom shuddering and saying, 'Oh, Mum. Please shut up. This is so gross.'

The only good thing about getting my period was that Mum did let me have the day off. Not all of my friends were allowed to have the day off. My mum felt sorry for me because I couldn't stop crying.

About an hour later, I walked to my mum's room to ask another question about sanitary towels and my dad was standing at the doorway.

He greeted me with, 'Oh, my little girl is a woman now.'

To say I was mortified is an understatement. I just flopped on my parents' bed and cried. It wasn't because I was thinking, 'Oh the joy of being a woman.' It was more like, 'Mum, I can't believe you told Dad. You arsehole.'

Becoming Americanised

CHAPTER FIVE

BEAUTY – YOU'LL HAVE YOUR DAY

Who wants to look like everyone else?

BEING so close to my brother Jack and also spending my childhood on the road with a bunch of guys meant I'd not really explored my feminine side as much as other girls my age. Getting my period made me think for the first time – but not in a cheesy way – 'Yeah, I'm a woman.'

Spending my teenage years in Los Angeles could be absolute agony at times. I was surrounded by all these gorgeous people who were constantly obsessed with their appearance. LA is about one thing only: perfection. Your face has to look incredible and your make-up immaculate. You're frowned upon if you're not near-to-death skinny and carrying the latest designer handbag.

There are places everywhere geared for plucking, preening, plumping... Everyone spends shit-loads on their appearance, from the average Joe to the top Hollywood stars. I refuse to buy into the idea that everyone has to look perfect. I really do. Who wants to look like everyone else? Everyone should strive to be an individual, not some Barbie doll clone.

At fourteen I started to get spots. Generally, I had good skin, but when I did get a spot it would be a really visible 'Hi, thanks for coming to join me on my face' type of spot. Everyone could see it. Forget the cover-up; this baby was going nowhere. I have pale skin too. A spot would always stand out like a big red traffic cone on my face. When it happened, all the boys at school would call me spotty. It was miserable. I'd turned fourteen in the October and by the New Year I'd had enough of people calling me spotty, even though I wasn't the only one who was called names. All the kids in my class were getting spots at some point.

One day after school, I went home to my mum and told her I was being picked on. She said we would sort it out. My mum was always available for advice on all stuff girly. If she was away with Dad she'd make sure she could be on the other end of the phone. Even today – and it doesn't matter where she is in the world – we can all call my mum up for a chat or advice.

Of course, in her line of work she's had to be tough. She's one of the few women who've made it in the music business and that doesn't come easy. But even though she's spent a lot of time with men, she's always very conscious of what the right clothes to wear are and her make-up is always immaculate too.

She took me on a shopping trip to the Beverly Center to help me buy some beauty products. I sat with a skin expert at the make-up store Aveda, where he talked me through a cleansing and moisturising regime that would help get rid of the spots. The shop was on the second floor, tucked away in the corner, which was great because it meant I didn't have to worry about bumping into my friends.

While we were in the Aveda store, my mum said I could have my own make-up set. I choose a six-by-six-inch box that flipped open. Inside, it had concealer, face powder, eye shadow and mascara. The make-up specialist told me how to use it. I'd been watching my sister Aimee, for ages, practising her make-up technique in front of the mirror at home. She'd bought a book from the department store, Barneys, and she would stand with the book opened on a certain page while she looked in the mirror and copied what they did.

The biggest arguments I used to have with my mum were over my sister. I always used to think that she spent more time with Aimee than she did with me. I wanted my mum to spend more time with me. When she was home, my mum took me, Jack and Aimee out on our own so we got plenty of one-on-one time with her. But sometimes I was jealous when she was with Aimee.

My sister is fucking beautiful. She really is beautiful. When we were kids, people would stop Mum in the street when we were all out shopping and tell her how beautiful Aimee was. Because I used to see myself as a bit goofy and a little chubby, I would say to mum, 'Why don't people look at me like they look at Aimee?'

Mum would always say to me, 'You'll have your day.' She told me that she had wanted me to learn how to wear make-up so I didn't repeat what she'd done. When Mum was my age, she had just gone out, bought a random kit and slapped it on. She ended up looking a real fucking tart.

77

That isn't to say I've not had my own make-up disasters. My God, the worst time was when I went to the MTV Europe Music Awards in Edinburgh in 2003, when I was nineteen. I swear to God, I don't know what the fuck I was thinking. My face is pale anyway, but I insisted on putting on this ridiculously white foundation. I then did the darkest eyes – I practically made them look like they'd sunk into my head. I then did the maddest, reddest lips ever. I looked like bloody Ursula Sea Witch – from *The Little Mermaid* movie. There are all these pictures of me on the red carpet with the singer Beyonce and I look fucking ridiculous. I thought I looked fantastic at the time.

I've been lucky enough to have had some amazing make-up artists do my make-up. I've tried to learn good tips along the way. Neil is the best I've ever worked with. He can look at anyone's face and know instantly what will work for their face shape and skin tone. I've never known him not do flawless make-up.

I was fifteen when I dyed my hair for the first time. We were staying at the Peninsula Hotel in New York. My dad was on tour and we'd flown out to join him. Dad's make-up artist and I were chatting in my parents' bedroom. I'd just had my hair cut really short and I loved it. But I was bored of the colour, which was blonde. She just said: 'Come on, Kel. Why don't we dye it?' I turned to my mum thinking she would say, 'No fucking way.' But she was really up for it. I'm not quite sure whether she was prepared for the colour I picked – bright pink! I loved it. And it was the start of my love affair with dying my hair. The only problem was, on my first day back at Westmark School after the holidays, they made me dye it back. The bastards!

Lino first started cutting my hair when I was two years old; I had to sit on my mum's knee because I was too small for the chair in the hairdresser's. He has been cutting my hair and my family's hair ever since. I am not kidding when I say that Lino has done the hair of every high-profile person you can think of – from Madonna and Kylie Minogue to Catherine Zeta Jones and Dustin Hoffman – and he won the award for the Most Wanted Cut & Blow Dry for styling my mum's hair. He was the head stylist on the first three series of *The X Factor* and he is now based at Daniel Galvin's hair salon in London.

THE biggest thing that pissed me off at school was when the other kids would always make a comment about how pale my skin was. They would turn around and say, 'Hi, Casper the Ghost'. You'd think they would come up with something better than that but no, they called me Casper. People still make reference to how I'm really pale now. I mean, never in a million years would they have dared to say, 'the blackest night' of a celebrity rapper. But they would have no problem saying, 'the ghostly white' of a celebrity rocker. No problem. Jesus fucking Christ! As if I can help the colour of my skin.

Those comments really hurt. No one wants to be picked on for something they can do absolutely nothing about.

I've worn fake tan twice in my life and I hated the way I looked on both occasions. Who is able to put that shit on properly? On

Beauty – You'll Have Your Day

the first occasion, I was going to one of Mum and Dad's parties and thought I would have a fake tan. I bought it from a store and attempted to do it myself. But you've got to exfoliate (remove the dead skin cells) and all that shit, which I'd not bothered to do. As soon as I'd done it, I freaked and decided I wanted to scrape it off. In the end I spent the night walking around the party with different coloured patches all over my chest. Nice.

Another time, I'd been on holiday and I had these weird strap-marks from where my swimsuit had been. I wouldn't have minded, but I'd been sitting in the shade. One of my friends told me to go to a beauty salon in LA and they would even it out. I stood in the middle of the room in some God-awful paper knickers while this woman sprayed my body with fake tan from a silver gun. I came out ten shades darker than I'd ever tan naturally. It just didn't look right and it really didn't suit me. I looked fucking ridiculous.

The problem with fake tans – and this was definitely the case with mine on that occasion – is they take on a life of their own after you leave the salon. They seem to change colour. I was very afraid of this, so I scrubbed that off too. I preferred the tan marks. I'm simply not meant for a tan. Everyone else in my family can tan, but I just don't tan at all. If I go into the sun, I get an awful heat rash. I burn really easily too. I really have to look after my skin. Now I'm pleased I can't sunbathe because sun really ages you. The last thing I want to look like is an old leather boot.

Mʏ first waxing experience was Home Waxing À La Sharon! My mother had only gone out and bought a home-waxing kit from a beauty store in the Beverly Center. We were living at North Beverly Drive and I was fourteen. My mum shouted from her bedroom, 'Kelly, my darling, come here.' I'd come to learn that those 'callings' would more than often mean, 'Hello, here comes trouble.'

My mum was standing in the middle of her bedroom, with this little pot that looked like it was bubbling. In her hand she was holding a plastic spatula. She said, 'Just lie down on your back for a minute.' I didn't have a clue what was going on. She then propped a towel under my head and another under my chin and over my T-shirt and jeans.

I was thinking, 'Oh my God. What the fuck is going to happen to me?'

She straddled herself across my stomach then proceeded to dip the spatula into the wax and smear it on my top lip. I screamed out in pain and my head involuntarily jerked up. My mum had heated the wax for too long and at too high a temperature. She didn't have a fucking clue what she was doing. Can you believe it? I was fourteen for God's sake. She was laughing her head off. I was lying back in absolute agony with a lump of congealed yellow wax sitting on my lip. I could barely move my mouth so I was mumbling to my mum, 'Oh my God. What the fuck have you done?' Mum was laughing so much, she wasn't concentrating, so when she finally got round to ripping off the wax it had stuck solid. After some small tugs at the corners, she did eventually pull it off. But half of my skin from my top lip went with it. I can't tell you how fucking painful it was. It was agony.

To make it worse, while I was wriggling around, my mum had pissed on me. She was laughing so hard that she couldn't keep the wee in. So as well as burning and scarring me, she also pissed on me. I stood up and I just knew. I knew. I walked over to the mirror and I had the biggest reddest mark ever on my top lip. I could hear my mum's distinct laugh in the background.

As the days went on, the scab grew. In the end, I was walking around school with the nastiest, biggest scab you've ever seen sitting under my nose. You know what? I'd actually like to say that everyone took the piss out of me at school. But they didn't. They all just felt sorry for me, which I think might have been worse. I'd tried to shrug the whole thing off by saying that I'd burnt my lip on a mug of chocolate. Yeah, one massive mug of hot chocolate. I don't think anyone believed me.

I now get my moustache waxed, even though it's what you'd call a 'milk moustache'. I don't want to be standing with someone and it catches the light and someone goes, 'Oh, look at Kelly's glistening blonde hair on her top lip.'

I WENT for my very first bikini wax at a fancy salon in Santa Monica. It was one of those places where you could get your fanny waxed into the shape of a butterfly or something crazy like that. I was really nervous and I didn't know what to expect. When I walked into the room she made me take off my knickers and put on those trusty paper knickers. I now understand that when it's done properly, the beautician has to pull your skin really tight

Fierce

as she yanks the wax strip in the opposite direction. The reason I know is because she didn't do that when she did mine. That first strip hurt so badly!

I hobbled out like bloody Charlie Chaplin. For days I was walking around with a fanny that looked like someone had kicked me between the legs. I was mortified. During those first few days, I winced every time I moved.

CHAPTER SIX

I WISH I'D WAITED

I didn't want to date anyone for a long time.
I just didn't trust anyone with my feelings.

OZZFEST was my favourite time of the year because we'd all get to go on the road with my dad. It was my summer camp. While all the other kids at my school, Westmark, were going off to camp to sail or play basketball or whatever, I was getting to hang out with some of the coolest rock bands in the world like Slipknot or System of a Down.

Mum and Dad had come up with the idea for Ozzfest in early 1996. It was a summer tour that started on the East Coast of America and finished on the West Coast. My parents decided to organise the festival when the organisers of a festival called Lollapalooza refused to let my dad join the tour. The first ever Ozzfest went on for just two days in October 1996, but from then it grew and grew. Over the years it's got bigger and bigger and has even come over to Europe to do some dates.

My parents' business manager Colin and his family would always travel from London for Ozzfest and that meant I got to hang out with Fleur, which was great because I didn't see as much of her after we'd moved to America.

The night before was always really exciting because we would all be frantically packing and deciding what to take, then hardly sleep for excitement and we'd all be wondering what the bus that we'd be sleeping on was like. Many of the people on the tour I'd not seen since the previous year, so it was one big get-together.

To give you an idea of how big Ozzfest had become after that first year in 1996, there were about sixty crew, twenty bands and two stages. It was for up-and-coming bands as well as established groups. Ozzfest has helped the career of many bands and singers like Marilyn Manson and Linkin Park. Jack and I would go around and cause chaos. I guess we were the kids of the organisers, so people used to hang out with us because they thought they could get away with murder. In the early days of Ozzfest it was all very innocent for me. It was like the best playground ever. I mean, the shit that we used to get into. People were always daring me to do things – and I'd always be the fucking one to do it.

Jack and I had these golf buggies that we drove around backstage. I used to do this thing where I'd wait for someone to go inside one of the portable toilets that would be lined up backstage. I'd wait until they'd locked the door and then I'd drive my golf cart straight into the loo. It would fall over, the door would bang open, and the poor guy inside would be lying there, covered in all the blue chemical shit that was in the toilet. I was so fucking naughty. I always used to feel really bad, but it was always so funny. The toilet would kind of rebound and stand back up again.

Fleur and I used to have the best fun. Jack and I would never let her drive the golf buggies because she was so shit at it. But there was one time when she'd asked us so many times, that we let her drive. She got in, put her foot on the accelerator, turned a corner, tipped over and just lay there on her side. She didn't drive again. We banned her.

When we first started going, I didn't give a shit about the bands. But I did watch my dad every night. That's always pretty special. Dad is such an amazing performer – when he gets on that stage he gives it one hundred per cent. He has the most amazing fans and he wants to make sure that they have the best night ever. Some people are born entertainers and my dad is one of them.

I met some friends for life at Ozzfest – one of them was Melinda. Her husband was a tour manager for one of the bands that was performing that year. After they got married, Aussie Melinda used to join him on the bus. I remember seeing her one day, reading a copy of *Heat* magazine that she'd got from the UK. I walked over to her and said, 'Oh my God, can I read your magazine?' She was about twenty-three then and we used to hang out all the time after that, reading magazines and making fun of the other people on the tour. Not long after, Mum was looking for a new nanny for us and I suggested Melinda. We all got on really well and I saw her as a big sister.

Many people will know Melinda from *The Osbournes*. She featured in the show – usually she was trying to get Jack out of bed or was telling us off for fighting.

Like so many people, she became a part of the family. She has always been there for me. When I'm in America she is the person I go to when I want advice if I'm not sure about going to my mum.

In 2008, she moved back home to Australia, but she still works for my family and manages to organise everything.

Following my initial lesson on sex when I was at primary school that had got me put into detention, my biggest sex education lesson came courtesy of Ozzfest. At every concert, there would be people handing out condoms and promoting safe sex to all the kids who would come along.

One year, Jack and I opened one of the packets and asked Mum what it was. She said, 'Don't ever have sex unless you use one of these.' That was it. I was too young to think about it, but because I'd grown up seeing condoms being handed out, safe sex wasn't a big deal for me. It was something my parents have never been shy about. They always told us what they thought and that we should protect ourselves.

Many years later, I agreed to front a campaign for World Contraception Day to raise awareness of what teenagers can do to prevent unwanted pregnancies, get the correct contraception and learn about sexually transmitted diseases.

I spoke quite candidly about some of the situations that I'd got myself into or how embarrassed I'd been in the past. Like the time I went into a Boots chemist in central London to buy some condoms and a newspaper wrote an article about it! I was so fucking mortified and for a long time I refused to buy them – I would send my flatmate instead. But then I thought, no, fuck this, I will buy them. Why should people feel embarrassed about buying condoms? I felt it was important to speak out.

Why should I feel self-conscious about protecting myself? That's the right thing to do. Or there was the time I thought I was pregnant when I'd not even had sex yet! I even did a test. That was pretty embarrassing too.

Boys can be real shits at times. I started dating a guy when I was fourteen. I think he was the first guy I kissed. I can't really remember, which shows just how memorable it was! It was all a bit childish really and it wasn't serious. We'd only been going out for a couple of weeks when he dumped me in front of everyone in the playground. His reason? He said I was fat. That really bloody hurt. He then started spreading these horrible rumours around school about me, like saying I was thick or something equally ridiculous. I went home from school one night really upset that this guy had been mean to me.

The next day, my mum turned up at school – I wasn't expecting to see her. The guy who'd dumped me was hanging out at the basketball court and she marched over. She tapped him on the shoulder and he turned around and she said, 'If you don't leave my daughter alone and stop saying nasty lies about her, I'm going to chop your dick off and shove it down your throat.'

It would be fair to say that no guy at school said horrible things about me again after that.

IWAS fifteen when I started to become sexually aware and I began to realise that boys were cool and not disgusting. We were all at Ozzfest. When we were on the tour we were all on different buses. Quite a lot of the teenagers were on our bus and anyone who had a teenage daughter or son would join us – it was chaos!

All the bands would have a different bus – there were loads of them. Each bus had a number. That was just for organisational reasons. Every year, we would put all the numbers into a hat, pick out a number and sleep in someone else's bus for the night. It was a great way of getting to know different people.

On this particular year, we played the game and I got the same bus as this guy who I really fancied and was in one of the bands that was performing. He was about seventeen or eighteen. We somehow ended up sleeping in the same bunk. You have to remember that I'd done a lot of my growing up on tour hanging out with the boys. So it wasn't a big deal for me to innocently share someone's bunk. But that soon changed . . .

We were lying there and he turned to me and asked, 'Has anyone ever licked your pussy?'

At this point, I'd never really kissed a boy properly. That word really frightened me – I don't fucking have a cat between my legs! There had been the guy at school, but we'd just pecked. My head was in the romantic clouds.

I said, 'What?' I didn't realise what he was talking about.

He wouldn't shut up. He kept saying, 'I love how you're so beautiful.'

And I was like, 'What the fuck are you talking about?'

Fierce

'

We were lying there and he turned to me and asked, "Has anyone ever licked your pussy?"

At this point, I'd never really kissed a boy properly. That word really frightened me – I don't fucking have a cat between my legs! There had been the guy at school, but we'd just pecked. My head was in the romantic clouds.

'

Then the penny dropped and I thought, 'Oh my God, he's talking about wanting to lick my fanny. Get me the hell out of here.'

I jumped straight out of the bunk and got into Jack's. I was absolutely mortified.

I still see this person to this day and now it's funny. It definitely wasn't then.

Some really fucked-up things happened to me on tour and some really amazing things – I guess that was one of the more fucked-up things.

W<small>HAT</small> I've always found funny is that older men are attracted to me. I can't figure out why. I've never been one of those girls who's walked around and said to some older woman, 'Hmmm, yeah, I bet I could have your husband.'

I like young and fresh. I'm not into old, grey and crusty. One of the reasons why some older guys might be attracted to me is because I've always been able to speak my mind – I'm way too old for my years. I think they like the idea of having a young girlfriend who can talk to them on the same level – either that or they don't want someone with saggy tits!

There was one time when I was nineteen when my dad and I were at a party. We were literally standing there holding hands when this guy in his forties came over and cupped my breasts in his hands. My dad whispered to me, 'Right, Kelly. That's it. We're going home.' Dad knew he couldn't do anything about it because it would make matters worse.

When I was at school, I always attracted the geeks in the

older years. It was usually the computer guys. Why? None of the other guys at school found me attractive. I knew that I wasn't going to find my one and only true love in high school, that's for sure.

One thing I really hated about going to school in America was that everyone is divided into groups. You've got the cool kids, the rich kids, the jocks, the stoners, the nerds . . . Me? I would be with the fat kids. Me, Molly and Tali would hang out together and try not to give a shit about the others. I was the only British girl at school, so I did stand out, but I didn't fancy any of the guys and I hated, hated the way that everyone was judged just because of the group they were in. I didn't fucking care! I didn't want to just hang around with people in one group. Who does that?

Actually, something I've always tried to do is to stay friends with everyone. Today I live by the same rule. Adulthood doesn't stop the petty arguments that can happen between friends, but I always keep well out of them. I don't want to get involved in other people's shit. I don't want to know. If someone wants my advice, fine. But I don't like the whole 'He said, she said' drama. It's absolute bullshit and I switch off.

I was never one of those girls who wanted to impress the boys. I didn't slap on the make-up before school or strut about in the classroom to get some guy's attention. That just wasn't me.

For a long time, and I think it's because I grew up on the road with my father and a bunch of guys, I used to look at relationships from a male point of view. I had a bit of a man's approach to going out with someone. Normally, when a couple

I Wish I'd Waited

break up, you would expect the girl to keep calling or be upset – if she wasn't the one to end it. But the guy would not give a shit. Even if the girl does the dumping, guys tend to have this macho image they want to protect and so try to move on quickly and not show they're bothered. I was a bit like that. But that all changed when I started to have proper relationships.

The first time I had sex I was sixteen, but I wasn't ready. I wasn't ready at all. I'd been going out with this guy for six months. He was eighteen, so he had his own apartment. We'd met in a club one night. Honestly, I slept with him because I thought it would make him stay with me. I sensed we might split up. That was such a stupid thing to do. I was sober, it wasn't particularly planned, but I'd sort of thought I should if we stayed together and it just happened one night. I was so nervous and worried.

The main thing was I just wasn't prepared for all the emotions and feelings that come with having sex with someone for the first time. To make matters worse, he dumped me the next day. He never spoke to me again. He dumped me because he wanted to be with someone else. Whether I'd had sex with him or not, he was always going to do that. I wish I'd waited.

It affected me so much that I didn't have sex again for a year. I couldn't bear to go through all the upset. Sex is not just about the physical act. As soon as you have sex, you have to think about having a cervical smear. It can detect the cells that could make you susceptible to cancer.

I had my sister, Aimee, to look out for me! I'm not sure if I'm grateful or not. Once, she booked an appointment with a gynaecologist to have my fanny checked – but didn't tell me. I only found out when I was with my mum on one of her shopping sprees in the jewellery store Tiffany &. Co. in Beverly Hills. I had my mobile on speakerphone when the call came through from the doctor's receptionist, who had called to confirm my appointment. It was announced to the whole of the store. I was so embarrassed. And then I was bloody annoyed. My fanny is no one's business. Not even my father's for that matter. As soon as he heard about it, he started questioning me in the kitchen about whether I'd had sex or not. There are some things you don't want your parents to know about.

I think it was really difficult for Mum to let go and accept that we were all growing up. She was so, so proud of us all. But her 'babies' had become teenagers. We'd all become more independent but even so, when I was fourteen, Mum still insisted on driving me everywhere. She'd never let me walk. She would drop me off and then tell me to call her and she'd come and pick me up. Sometimes it was embarrassing.

Mum has always been a real mum's mum. Yes, my mum and dad are incredibly successful. It would kill me if I tried to emulate the kind of success they've had in their careers. Really, I couldn't. Sometimes I panic when I have to fill out a form and I get to the bit when it says: 'What's your occupation?' I never know what to put. But I think that if you asked Mum and Dad what they'd count as their biggest achievement, they'd say, 'Our children.' Mum would probably put it down as her occupation too!

My mum loved being at home with her babies. But the trouble was we were all in our teens and growing up quickly. We wanted

I Wish I'd Waited

to do our own stuff with our friends. Mum would always be hovering in the doorway of my bedroom desperate to join in. It was even worse when my friends came over. Mum loved being one of the girls. I just used to find it so embarrassing. She would come and lie on my bed next to my friends and join in all the conversations about make-up and boys. Stuff you really don't want your mum to know about.

I was always saying to her, 'Get out, Mum.' Molly and Tali sometimes couldn't believe how abrupt I was being to my mum. But that just sums up everything about living in Los Angeles.

It was another reason why I didn't like it. In the UK, if I'd done something stupid or pissed someone off, they would always say, 'Kelly, you have annoyed me. You're being an idiot. Shut up or fuck off.' I liked that. You knew where you were. When my mum annoyed me, I told her. In Los Angeles, so many people just sit there when someone is being annoying and don't say shit. They just smile and try to appease them. I was always meant to live in the UK. British humour suits me and I like the directness that people have. My mum used to just laugh and wind me up even more when I got annoyed with her. She'd come up to me and try and hug and kiss me in front of my friends. She'd say stuff like, 'Oh, Kelly, your friends want to hang out with Kelly's mummy.'

I swear to God, my mum is going to be the craziest grandma because she just loves babies. She is an incredible hoarder. She's kept absolutely everything from our childhoods. Back at Welders, my mum has a box in her dressing room full of all the shoes we used to wear. There isn't just mine, Aimee's and Jack's first pair of shoes there. I could almost understand that. No,

'Oh Kelly,

your friends want to hang out

with Kelly's mummy'

there are our second pair of shoes, our third pair of shoes. There are shoes in there that I had when I was six. She would never in a million years dream of throwing something out. Not even a hanky we'd probably once blown our nose on.

Do you want to know what one of the worse things about getting older is? You end up turning into your mother. I realised this when I was about fifteen. For a start, we have the same laugh. My dad would always say to me and Mum, 'You two will never be lonely because of your laugh. It's so infectious that people will always want to be around you.' It isn't only our laugh though. We have the same size feet and hands. Our facial mannerisms are very similar too. I would love to be a successful businesswoman like my mum – when she walks into a room, she has a real presence. I think that's fantastic. Although, when she's in a bad mood, we all bloody know about it too. At times it was difficult because my mum would want to be our friend, but then she would go ape-shit if we went out too late. She was always screaming, 'Why do you have to go out every night? You can't wear that. Why are you wearing that? Why are you putting that make-up on your face? Who's that you're hanging out with?' It used to drive me absolutely insane. And then, when I started hanging out with guys, Mum wanted to be the other woman in the relationship. Not in a sick way. But because she cares so much she always wants to be a part of my life. But you just don't want your mum hanging out with you when you're with a boy. Never!

Fucking hell, I've had my heart broken. Hell, yeah. At the time it was the most horrendous thing I have ever experienced.

The first time was when I was nineteen. I was dating a singer called Bert McCracken. He was in a band called The Used and I met him when I was seventeen and he was performing with his band at Ozzfest. It was my first serious relationship and it was during the time that we were filming *The Osbournes*, so the whole world seemed to know about Bert and me.

He was the first guy I'd really loved. I was so hung up on him. It was Valentine's Day and the cameras were in our house. It was my first big Valentine's Day and because he was on tour, I was

Fierce

thinking I would get flowers delivered. He called me up and said to me the stupidest thing that anyone has ever said to me in my whole fucking life. He said, 'You know, Happy Valentine's Day, baby. You're so beautiful. You know you're so great. I am so glad I met you and you WERE in my life. One day you will be in that white dress walking down the aisle with me.

'But you know, we can't date right now because I just want to ROCK!' He actually screamed 'rock!' like he was at a concert on stage or something. He continued: 'I just want to fucking ROCK!'

At that precise point, I just wanted to take a bag full of rocks and bash his fucking head in. That's what I wanted to do. But the pain of being dumped on Valentine's Day didn't end there. He then came out with, 'The thing is, people don't take me seriously because I date you. All I want to do is ROCK!' That last sentence 'People don't take me seriously because I date you,' took away four years of my life. I was so unbelievably upset.

Instead of laughing at how stupid he'd sounded saying he just wanted to rock, I concentrated on the criticism about me. It sent me on a downward spiral of self-hatred. It sent me insane – I just kept agonising over why people wouldn't take him seriously if he dated me. I was so terribly distressed and I didn't want to date anyone for a long time after that. I just didn't trust anyone with my feelings.

Who the fuck says that to someone? I had to walk back down the stairs and into the kitchen at Doheny and have the MTV cameras capture me saying I had been dumped on Valentine's Day. I tell you, it was bloody humiliating and upsetting. And

'I wish I'd known

Amy Winehouse in those days.

Believe it or not,

she gives the best fucking advice.'

because of the show, the whole world knew about it. There was no running away.

Now I laugh about it. It was like a scene from the mockumentary *Spinal Tap* which took the piss out of a rock band. After that phone call, I never saw or spoke to Bert again. In the early days I wouldn't have known whether to have hugged or punched him if I'd bumped into him.

Now, I wish him the best life has to offer. He taught me that I was capable of loving someone who was outside of my family. Looking back though, I can't actually think of one single thing that we did together that I thought was fun. I don't even know why we dated in the first place. I really don't. I wish I'd known Amy Winehouse in those days. Believe it or not, she gives the best fucking advice.

Years later, when I was living in London and we'd become friends, Amy really made me look at heartbreak in a different way. I'd been seeing a guy for nearly two years, who I really fucking liked. He was in a band that was doing well. We had first met in Monaco – we hung out and got on really well. I'd never met anyone who I'd clicked with like I did with him. Anyway, it turned out that he'd been lying to me about being single and I was so upset. That's when it started to get, as the Facebook status says, 'complicated'. I was the idiot who had sat around for two years thinking he would go out with me.

Amy had come round to my house one afternoon and she was so great. She said to me, 'Kel, you've got to look at it like this: whatever you had with him, no one can take it away. You had that with him.'

I thought, you're right. It ended in a shitty way, but the good times no one would be able to take away. It instantly made me feel better and helped me move on.

Deep down, all Amy wants to do is have a family, settle down and be left the fuck alone. That girl is not stupid.

I Wish I'd Waited

CHAPTER SEVEN

THE LESSER OF MY VICES

Growing up with an alcoholic wasn't enough to stop me wanting to try alcohol.

WHEN I was growing up, I was adamant I would never drink alcohol because of my dad's problem with booze; it felt like I'd been put off for ever. Unfortunately, life doesn't always work out like that. And even though I grew up to not have a major problem with alcohol (bottles of wine can stay in my house for months and I don't drink them if I don't want them), I did develop my own vices that would make me more understanding of my father's addictions.

When I was a kid, I didn't know what the future held, so I often felt very angry about my dad's drinking habits. When he wasn't getting high on drugs, he'd be going through a period when he would be drinking a lot. He'd start off being someone who was cool to be around. But after a period on the booze it would make him angry and difficult. When we were living at

Welders, if Dad wasn't on tour, we'd get the full force of his addiction to alcohol and it wasn't always pleasant, believe me.

My mum did her very best to shield us from my father's drunken behaviour, but there were just some things she couldn't stop us seeing. When you're the child of someone who has a drink problem, it turns you into the parent. That should never happen. One afternoon Dad had got really drunk and puked everywhere. I was trying to get him to drink some water. Crouching on my knees on the floor next to my parents' bed, I was holding the glass to his lips and encouraging him to drink it as he lay there. It was really stressful. I had all these emotions like, is this my fault? Why is he doing it? Is there something I can do to make it better? It was hard at times, really hard.

My mum always made sure we were very informed about what was going on and what everything meant and what someone had to do in order to get better. She would sit us down in the kitchen and say to us, 'Your father is an alcoholic.' Then she would tell us what that meant. My definition of alcoholism is a whole bunch of things: disruption, worry, hope . . . it isn't as simple as saying it's just drinking too much. There's so much more to it.

When I was nine my mum got a doctor to come and visit us at home at Welders and he sat and explained what it meant to be an alcoholic. We could ask any question we wanted. That really helped and I think it was really brave and right that my mum did that. Sometimes it takes an authority figure other than your parents to explain something that at the time seems so complicated.

Fierce

That's not to say that, in the past, I haven't got really angry with my dad for his drinking. There was one afternoon when we were living in America, not long after we'd started filming *The Osbournes* that I just lost it. I turned around to my dad, who was drunk and standing in the middle of the kitchen at Doheny, and screamed, 'You know what, you're absolutely pathetic. I am fucking sick of this. You're a shit father.'

I was angry, upset and I'd had enough. He came towards me, but his security guard pulled him back and my mum grabbed a wooden candlestick and went to hit him over the head with it. When my mum told him what had happened the next day when he'd sobered up he cried. He cried for two days. He just couldn't believe what had happened. He couldn't remember it.

I love my dad more than anything. Now, more than ever, I understand how hard it is to fight an addiction. I don't blame him or hate him. I feel sad it happened. I thought my dad was going to die all the time from drink and drugs. I still have that fear, even though he has been clean since 2003. But I'm so proud of him. He did it – it's not easy, but he did it – and although every day is a struggle for him, he's stayed clean.

Growing up with an alcoholic wasn't enough to stop me wanting to try alcohol when I was thirteen. It was around this time that I got drunk for the first time. We were on holiday in Hawaii. We always used to go there when we moved to

The Lesser Of My Vices

America. We were away with another family, and one of their kids had got hold of a bottle of vodka. We told our parents we were going swimming and left the hotel. In another resort nearby we sat in a circle on the beach and starting drinking. I felt so grown up and cool. Apart from the odd sip of champagne at Christmas when I'd usually spit it out, I'd never tasted alcohol and I was intrigued. I'm not joking. Jack, who was only twelve, gave me the equivalent of two tablespoons of vodka in a small glass – and I was pissed out of my head! I whispered to Jack that I didn't feel well and he had to help me to bed. There would be many similar scenarios to come. I was the older sister and I was meant to be the one looking out for him. The whole time he was saying, 'Don't worry, Kelly, you're just feeling a little bit drunk. You'll feel OK once you've slept it off.' I couldn't believe that my little brother was teaching me what being drunk was all about. We were sharing a bedroom, so he put me to bed and sat on the floor next to my bed until I started to feel a bit better. The next day I felt like shit. I suppose it was my first-ever hangover. It's a bit embarrassing really, bearing in mind how much I'd drunk.

I worried about my father and knew what alcohol could do, but I didn't associate it with my own experimentation. Put it this way, witnessing my father's battles with alcohol was not enough to stop me experimenting, which is what a lot of young people are doing. They're experimenting.

When we moved to America, all the kids at school would have parties in their parents' mansions in Beverly Hills. I would get a text on my phone on a weekend saying 'house party' with the address and we would all drive over.

Fierce

In California, you can get your provisional driving licence when you're fifteen and a half. That means you can drive a car with a licence holder for six months before taking your test when you're sixteen.

Uncle Tony used to take me out all the time around LA so I could practise. At the time, my dad had a crazy Irish security guard who was ace. He took me out for my first-ever lesson. I was sitting in the driving seat and gripping the wheel – I was absolutely shitting myself. Meanwhile, he was jabbering away next to me about how people shouldn't need to use electric toothbrushes, but should instead brush their teeth themselves.

I was muttering to myself, 'Electric toothbrushes? Hmm, do they have something to do with driving a car?'

I passed the test first time. Mum and Dad bought me a black Chrysler PT Cruiser with flames. Whenever there was a party, I'd pick up Molly and Tali and we'd head over. Everyone at school got shit cars – especially the girls. They all wanted to look like the 'booty girls' who appeared in rap videos and hung out in big fuck-off convertibles. They'd all be driving these massive cars – they looked ridiculous.

I hated going to 'school parties'. It was the same time and time again. The party was always at some massive house, usually the parents were away and the police would always be called because the neighbours had complained about the noise or something. They'd walk in and I'd be standing thinking, 'I really hate this. I really don't want to be here.'

There was always alcohol there, but I never used to drink. I never felt under pressure to drink at those parties anyway. I didn't want to be the person puking in the corner who everyone would be talking about at school on the Monday. No way! Someone would always bring a keg of beer and all the guys would be drinking that. Meanwhile, all the girls would be sipping on some gross peach schnapps. It all felt so juvenile.

The girls were usually blonde and they'd all be wearing UGG boots, Juicy Couture tracksuits, and popping chewing gum and saying, 'Oh my God.' Sad-arsed motherfuckers! And the guys; they'd swagger intothe party and I'd be thinking: 'Just because you have the Michael Jordan jersey on and you've stolen your dad's expensive watch doesn't make you look cool. And you're talking like you're black when you couldn't be more white. In fact you're practically albino. You're not hot!'

I absolutely hated what those parties represented. I really did. They were so gossipy and the people who were there actually cared about who was snogging who – who gave a shit? I didn't.

ON Sunset in West Hollywood there's a hotel called The Hyatt, but it's nicknamed The Riot House. Back in the seventies and eighties, all these rock bands used to stay in it and completely trash it. Just up the road is another hotel called The Sunset Marquis. It's the hotel where lots of musicians and bands hang out. They used to trash their rooms at that hotel too. They did it because they thought it made them cool; it didn't.

Before we moved into *The Osbournes'* house on Doheny Road, we stayed at The Sunset Marquis. There was the main

Fierce

‘

I was muttering to myself,

"Electric toothbrushes?

Hmm, do they have **something to do**

with driving a car?"

’

hotel and then there were individual apartments. We were in one of the apartments that was in the middle of grounds full of flowers and cut grass – it was really nice. My bedroom stunk of mothballs though, which was a bit weird because otherwise it was a really nice place.

There was a recording studio in the hotel, which is why it was so popular with musicians, and there was this really cool bar called The Whiskey Bar. My father had been staying at that hotel with my mum since the early Black Sabbath days.

While we were living there I would go down to The Whiskey Bar in my pyjamas – they were like the ones Ally McBeal wore on the television show. I'd sneak out and climb down the balcony without my parents knowing.

The manager used to let me sit behind the bar and clean the glasses for him. There was a massive black-and-white picture of my dad on one of the walls. It was only a small bar, but loads of people used to hang out there. It had a really nice atmosphere and the bar used to run across the entire room on the back wall opposite the entrance. I'd be sitting there in my pyjamas chatting to all the musicians. Noel and Liam Gallagher sat there when I was behind the bar a few times. They were cool and chatted to me. Another night Eminem came in and Slash from Guns N' Roses. It was a laugh. The barmen, who became my friends, would be passing me glasses of pineapple juice, but my parents didn't know they were putting in shots of Malibu. It was the first time that I drank socially.

It wasn't long before we started filming *The Osbournes* and Jack and I really hated going to school. We just didn't want to go. We were always hanging off the balcony of our whitewashed apartment in the morning chucking stuff off and saying, 'We're not going to school.'

The Welsh actor Rhys Ifans was staying in the hotel at the time because he was filming the movie *Little Nicky*.He used to piss himself laughing at us when he walked past to go to the studio. He thought we were mad, out of-control kids! On his days off from filming, he used to come and hang out with us. Rhys is a really cool and funny guy. Years later we became good friends when I moved to London and we would hang out together with Kate Moss and Davinia Taylor.

WHEN I was fourteen, I started going to a club called On The Rox. It was above The Roxy, which is a famous club on Sunset. Loads of people would hang out there but, basically, it was a room above the club where the owners would hang out. My parents knew them really well – they used to go there when they were younger. Even though you had to be twenty-one to get in we didn't have any problems because my mum knew everyone there. Her theory was that if she let us go out, at least she knew where we were and that we were going to be safe.

I swear to God my mum had spies on us when we were there because when I'd get home she'd know exactly who I'd spoken to and what I'd drunk. I'd walk in at midnight and she'd say, 'Kelly, you've been drinking.'

I'd say, 'I've not had a drop.'

But she would come back with, 'I know you've had two Malibu pineapples.' I couldn't get away with anything.

The Lesser Of My Vices

The great thing about On The Rox – especially after *The Osbournes* show started and we would get bothered all the time – was that it was up to the owners who got in. Sometimes there would be 300 people queuing to get in, but there would only be five people inside. I used to hang out with Jack there and my friends Molly and Tali. One time when Sammy and Fleur were visiting from the UK, I took them there. Sammy got so drunk she thought she was a sheep! A fucking sheep! She had one of those denim jackets on that had sheep's wool on the inside and it kind of fucked with her head because she'd drunk so much. That was one of the funniest nights I ever spent there.

On The Rox was really cool – it had lots of secret rooms. Rumour has it that the legendary Hollywood madam Heidi Fleiss used to entertain some of her men in those rooms. Who knows, but it's a fucking good tale to tell.

I always used to drink Malibu pineapple then. It was my favourite drink. One night I drank seven. One minute I was sitting there laughing with everyone, the next the room was spinning. And I mean really spinning. You know that ride you can go on at the fair where you all stand with your back against a wall and the floor moves and the pressure keeps you sucked to the wall, but your head feels heavy? Well, that's exactly how I felt. My head felt so fucking heavy. Every time I put it up it felt like I was going to fall over. I felt so ill. Fortunately, Doctor Jack came to the rescue. My little brother Jack is an expert on everything. As soon as he's read a paragraph on anything he becomes man-in-the-know. I turned to him and said, 'Jack, the room is spinning. I don't feel very well.'

'He put me to bed – again –

and I lay there looking up at the ceiling

thinking that I was going to die.

Jack lay next to me the whole night.

It wasn't until 8 a.m.

that I finally stopped freaking out. '

In the taxi on the way home with me lolloping all over the back seat, he told me he suspected I had alcohol poisoning. It was totally the wrong thing to say to me because straight away I thought I was going to die. I was screaming out, 'Oh my God, I'm going to die of alcohol poisoning.' He was just sitting there stroking my arm.

He put me to bed – again – and I lay there looking up at the ceiling thinking that I was going to die. Jack lay next to me the whole night. It wasn't until 8 a.m. that I finally stopped freaking out.

It was just before *The Osbournes* started that I was first introduced to Nicole Richie. I was at The Standard Hotel, which is also just on Sunset. There is a bar through the restaurant at the front called The Purple Lounge. Nicole knew a friend of mine and she came over and said to me, 'Oh my God, you're so cute.' She's older than me, but when I used to see her out and about we'd hang out. Paris Hilton and Nicole have known each other for years. I met Paris on a separate occasion. I can remember it really well because it was the night the R&B singer Aaliyah died in a plane crash which was in August 2001. It was at a house party and Paris was standing on a table holding on to a window sill and dancing. I noticed that her tit kept falling out of her dress and she'd not realised because she was drunk. Loads of people around her were taking pictures. I felt like she was being taken advantage of, so I went up to her and put the sleeve back up on her blue dress. We've been friends ever since. I think Paris is a lot cleverer than people give her credit for.

I was with Paris when I suffered one of the worse hangovers I've ever had. It was just before my twenty-first birthday. A whole bunch of us had driven from Los Angeles to Vegas. We'd gone out for dinner and then to have a few drinks. I had just a couple of glasses of martinis at dinner and then we went to a club and I did about three shots. Almost as soon as I'd downed the final shot I was throwing up. I didn't stop throwing up until the next day. I thought I was going to die. I really did.

On the day I got a fake ID card from downtown Los Angeles, I got alcohol poisoning for real! I'd had a massive fight with my mum and dad. I can't even remember what it was about, which just goes to show that big fights count for shit when you're older.

We were living at Doheny Road and I went storming out of the kitchen and into my bedroom. I was crying and I was pissed off. I packed a bag and called a friend of mine to come and pick me up. When she pulled up outside I was still sobbing. She turned to me and said: 'Kel, you need to calm down. You're smudging your eye make-up.'

She handed me a Xanax, which is a drug that's given to people who suffer from panic attacks and anxiety. I'd never even heard of Xanax before, but I took one of the pills and instantly it made me feel loads calmer.

In the end, I'd forgotten that I'd even taken it. I was drinking and I didn't give it a second thought that I'd taken a Xanax. That night I got so unbelievably drunk. My hairdresser actually found me in the grounds outside The Standard, passed out. She recognised me by my sparkly shoes that were poking out of the bush I'd fallen into right near a bus stop. How embarrassing is

The Lesser Of My Vices

this story? I don't know how I got there and I don't know what had happened to my friends. But mixing Xanax with alcohol was obviously not a very good idea.

My hairdresser helped me up and drove me home. As soon as I walked through the door I collapsed. Mum and Jack took one look at me and drove me to the Cedars-Sinai , a private LA hospital, where I had my stomach pumped. I can't remember what they did to me, but I felt so unbelievably sick. Mum and Jack stayed with me and then they drove me home and I just fell into in bed. I felt so bloody weak. Every part of my body ached. My head was thumping.

The next day, I was in the foulest mood ever. I can't remember who it was, but someone came into the kitchen when I was making some tomato soup to try and make myself feel better. Whoever it was was trying to give me a lecture on drinking too much. I just got the bowl of tomato soup and threw it at the wall. I'm not proud of doing that, but I think I just felt so angry and pissed off that I'd got myself into that situation. I didn't need to hear it.

ALCOHOL is the lesser of my vices. But when there isn't anything else, that's what I turn to. I can drink anyone under the table. The problem with being in the public eye is that you can no longer go out and drink without there being a picture in the paper the next day. That has happened to me so many times. And sometimes I've not even been that pissed, but all a photographer needs to do is snap you while you're blinking and you instantly look like you've had too much to drink.

Fierce

'I just got the

bowl of

tomato soup

and threw it at the wall.'

In May 2008, there were the most embarrassing pictures ever of me plastered all over the papers. They had a profound effect on me. I'd been out drinking every single night that week so I probably should have stayed in on this one night, when I'd gone to see a band at Koko in Camden with a whole bunch of girlfriends. Afterwards we went to the nightclub Mahiki which is known for its Treasure Chest Cocktails. Before then, I'd had a shot of sambuca. I have no idea what's in a Treasure Chest, but you all sit around it with your straws sticking out. It tasted fruity and it went straight to my head. Afterwards, when we left the club, it was just chaos. There were photographers everywhere and they were pushing and I was unsteady on my feet.

I don't have a problem with the media – they're doing their jobs and they're usually very nice about me. But there are times when the photographers push you and shout out nasty things to get a reaction. On this night I was being bumped all over the place. Sometimes, no matter how politely you ask them to get out of your way, they don't get out of your way. When I've had a couple of drinks I just say to myself, 'Keep your head down, Kelly. Keep your head down.'

The next day I just knew I was going to get a hammering in the papers. There were headlines that said: 'Drunk Kelly's Legs Go to Jelly.' Another one said: 'Kelly's a bit Peaky in Mahiki.' Those pictures absolutely destroyed me, they really did. It was a valuable lesson learned. I didn't go out drinking for a while after that. I felt so ashamed.

The Lesser Of My Vices

KELLY OSBOURNE

CHAPTER EIGHT

VICODIN

I thought I'd found my magic remedy.

WHEN we were little (and usually just after he had just spent time in rehab and was sober) Dad would gather me, Jack and Aimee together and sit us down and tell us very seriously, but in a calm voice, 'One of you, if not all of you, will have "the gene".'

I must have been about eight years old when Dad first started saying this to me. I didn't have a clue what he meant. I was aware that my father was an alcoholic and addicted to drugs because there were no secrets in our house. My mum believed in telling us the truth, but the whole 'gene thing' I didn't get at all.

Of course, now I realise what my dad was trying to tell us was that he feared one of us would inherit the gene that made someone an addict just like he was, and it was very much on his conscience. As he battled his addictions to drink and drugs, he was very frightened one of his children would follow him down the same destructive path when they got older. He had no idea what they might be addicted to because it isn't just about drink or drugs. You can be addicted to anything from gambling to tomato soup.

I didn't feel scared for myself when my dad talked to us about addiction like this because I was too busy worrying about him. I'm not joking when I say that I'd regularly come home from school at 3.30 p.m. when we were living at Welders and find my dad, passed out on the big comfy sofa in the kitchen because he'd drunk too much during the day. He'd be sprawled out snoring his head off after falling off the wagon yet again, as family life went on around him. We'd be chatting to Mum about our homework and Dad would be lying there completely out of it.

Other times, he'd be sitting upright chattering to anyone who'd listen because he'd taken cocaine and was as high as a kite. That was a normal scenario for me and it made me so scared for him. I was terrified that something bad would happen. Kids, even at the age of eight, are very perceptive. That's why I spent the whole time worrying about my dad.

The first time I really thought about my Dad's 'gene talk' and really got what he was trying to tell us was when I was thirteen. It wasn't long after we'd moved to LA permanently and I started to suffer from sore throats. I was eventually diagnosed with tonsillitis and the doctors decided that I should have my tonsils taken out instead of suffering the agony of the excruciating needle-stabbing pain in my throat at regular intervals throughout the year.

I was admitted into Cedars-Sinai in the summer of 1998 and my mum took me in for the operation and a one-night stay. The surgery was over quickly, and afterwards I got to stay in my own room while I recovered. It was while I lay there in bed with the sun shining through the window that I realised I might have an issue with drugs. The doctors had prescribed liquid Vicodin, a strong painkiller only available in America; it's mainly given to patients who have had oral or dentistry operations but you can take it for other things too. The nurses would pop by my room and give me a little capful every so often and it would help numb the pain from the operation. I didn't think I was taking a drug because it was just a medicine to me. But for the first time since we'd moved to Los Angeles, whenever I swallowed that tiny dose of medicine I felt relaxed and contented. Liquid Vicodin seemed to take away the stress of living in another country. I was prescribed two weeks' worth while I recovered at home on North Beverly Drive and I thought, 'I like the feeling this drug gives me.'

When the two-week prescription ran out, there was no more access to liquid Vicodin so that was the end of that. Then, years later, when I was sixteen, I started going to a nightclub called Las Palmas, just off Hollywood Boulevard. It was the summer of 2001, just before we started filming *The Osbournes* that October. The club was very close to The Sunset Marquis hotel, where we were staying in an apartment while we waited to move into our new home on Doheny Road. We were staying in a whitewashed three-bedroom apartment that was next to the main entrance. I remember it overlooked a side street and I shared a bedroom over the garage with Aimee.

Wednesday was Las Palmas night and on this particular night I'd gone alone and planned to meet my friends inside.

It was around this time that Jack had also told me he didn't want to hang out with me any more. I used to turn up at the same nightclubs as him and he'd scream in the queue at me, 'Kelly, I don't want you coming here. What are you doing here? I discovered it first.' We would have terrible, terrible fights. We'd always been so close, but all of a sudden we were arguing night and day. It broke my heart.

Jack was fifteen and had started drinking and experimenting with cannabis; he was using them to escape the anxieties he was feeling. It would seem Jack had 'the gene'. I knew what he was doing - we were both experimenting with drugs – and I think that's why we started to argue because we simply couldn't bring ourselves to talk about it. That was weird because we'd always confided in each other about everything.

On loads of occasions, Jack would march into the house at the end of a night out and go and wake up my mum and say, 'Kelly's out of order, Mum. She abandoned me in a nightclub.' But the truth was he'd told me he hadn't wanted me around him and his friends. I couldn't win.

I started hanging out with my own friends, but Jack and I would always end up in the same places because that's what LA's like and there was a limit to the number of clubs we could get into because Jack was fifteen and I was sixteen and we were well under the LA age limit of twenty-one to drink and get into nightclubs. I knew a whole bunch of people at Las Palmas and most people were underage, but no one gave a shit. The show hadn't started yet and everyone in the club knew me for me, not Kelly Osbourne from *The Osbournes*. I'd driven myself there in

'*It didn't scare me.*

It reassured me. So I took a small

white pill out of the bottle and

swallowed it back with my drink.'

my black 4x4 – I'd passed my test to drive an automatic car – no one walks in Los Angeles. Walk somewhere? Are you joking?

I pulled up outside the club that was about a five-minute drive from the hotel and parked on the road. It was around 11 p.m., noisy and hot inside. I talked to the people I knew while I sat at a table with my sour-apple martinis, which I always ordered. An hour or so went by, then this guy, who I'd never seen before and who was older than me, leaned over his friend and said, 'Hey, do you want one of these?'

I didn't have a clue what he was offering, but when I looked down in his hand he was holding a prescription bottle full of pills. The bottle had similar writing to the sticky label that had been on the outside of the bottle of liquid Vicodin that I'd taken when I'd had my tonsils out. It didn't scare me. It reassured me. So I took a small white pill out of the bottle and swallowed it back with my drink.

I wasn't stupid. I'd been brought up with a father who had taken every drug available to him – including Vicodin – and I knew some of my friends smoked cannabis. But I'd not really thought about taking drugs myself. After swallowing the little white pill I very quickly felt like I could talk to anyone. I was relaxed and happy and a bit tingly. It was the same feeling I'd experienced when I was thirteen and in that hospital bed. I knew it was Vicodin. In an instant it stopped me feeling self-conscious and I thought, 'I've found my magic remedy.' I wanted more.

I was still enjoying the effects of the Vicodin when I got back to the hotel apartment in the early hours and it felt good. In fact, for the first time in months I felt happy. When I woke up the next morning, the effects had worn off, but I'd taken the number of the guy who'd given it to me so I called it from my bedroom on my mobile phone. Straight away he agreed to meet me and I waited for him on the street.

I only bought two or three pills and planned to take them the next time I went out. They cost me about twenty dollars. I kept the Vicodin pills I'd bought in my bag and took them the following week. I swallowed one with water before going out. The effects of one tablet lasted the whole night and made me feel more confident. Soon my life was going to change and I'd come to rely on Vicodin more and more.

CHAPTER NINE

THE OSBOURNES

*It did start to freak us out. When people are being so
kind to you all the time you wonder what they want.*

About a year after we'd moved to LA in 1999, MTV visited our house on North Beverly Drive to record an episode of *Cribs*. It was a TV show that had been running for some time. They went into the home of some celebrity and filmed inside and then always made a big issue of their huge fridge and their fancy cars. Mum wasn't in it, but Jack, Dad and I did it and it was cool, but we didn't give it much more thought and a year passed.

MTV had contacted us because a few months earlier, a production company had come to film us all for a one-off documentary-style show called *Ozzy Osbourne Uncut*. It went on to win the Rose d'Or at the Montreux International Film Festival. Then came more interest in my family from other production companies.

After the MTV show had gone out, we found out that our episode had become the most requested show on MTV. I knew people would love my dad when they saw it. It had been an opportunity for them to find out what we'd known all our lives: my dad is fucking funny. At home, my dad would always be coming out with stuff that'd make us stop in our tracks and say in harmony, 'What?' and then we'd all just piss ourselves laughing. Yeah, my dad is famous and yeah, he's successful, but he's also just a working-class lad and always will be. I was so happy that people had loved that episode. Afterwards, my mum had a whole bunch of meetings with MTV, but we didn't take much notice. Then she said she wanted us all to meet the crew.

One night during the summer of 2001, she took us for dinner at Ivy at the Shore, which is the beach version of the famous Ivy restaurant in London and overlooks the sea in Santa Monica – just a few miles from Los Angeles. We'd go there a lot and it's a real family place. There's the pier where Forrest Gump ended his famous run across America and Muscle Beach where all the buff boys work out with weights on the sand. Arnold Schwarzenegger used to train there when he was bodybuilder.

All the MTV executives were waiting to meet us on the patio entrance overlooking the sea and me, Mum, Dad, Aimee and Jack went over and introduced ourselves. They explained to us a concept they had for a TV show in which they'd film us all at home. It would be a sort of extended *Cribs*.

Mum turned to us and said, 'It's up to you, would you like to do it?'

Straight away Jack and I said, 'Yes.'

Fierce

I thought to myself, this is going to be so cool, so fucking amazing. My friends and I watched MTV all the time and now my family were going to be on it!

I understood it to be a show primarily about my dad because he's bloody entertaining. We were simply giving our permission to let them film us in the background. Of course I wanted to take part behind the scenes, and I was cool if I appeared on screen now and again. I thought I would be the daughter no one would remember.

We all left the meeting really excited but Aimee had decided that she didn't want to appear front of camera. She's remained out of the spotlight ever since. It was October 2001 and we were just about to move into our new house on Doheny Road so the MTV film crew started filming on the day we moved in. Mum and Dad had bought the house from the King of Bongo who'd had to move back to Africa 'very quickly'. Mum being mum (she's not happy unless she's moving house or making her mark on a house) was in the process of gutting the place. She was ripping out pillars and making rooms bigger and knocking down walls. The builders were still finishing the work when we were moving in and it was chaos.

As you walked through the main door (she had all the original door handles taken off and replaced in the style of a cross), the staircase to the bedrooms sat in the middle of the oval entrance. In the far left-hand corner of the hallway were stable barn-style doors that led to the kitchen and small lounge. In one sense, the house appeared quite gothic with skulls and crosses hanging up. But then my mum would shove in a Laura Ashley-style sofa covered in flowers with matching lampshades and curtains. My mum's desk with her computer was in the kitchen too so that room was the centre of the house. The doors from the kitchen led to the garden, so the dogs would be in and out. My dad would be walking about moaning, 'Fuck me, I'm living in Doctor Dolittle's house. There's piss and shit everywhere.'

At first, I was really conscious of the cameras. I mean, who wouldn't be? I was convinced I wouldn't appear a lot so I wanted to make sure that when I did, I looked OK. I definitely made sure I put make-up on.

On that first day, my mum was on the driveway, hidden behind the heavy electronic wooden gates surrounded by hundreds of cardboard boxes with labels on saying: 'Kelly', 'Jack', 'lounge', 'kitchen', etc.', written in thick pen. She was busy directing the removal men. I was in my bedroom with our nanny Melinda unpacking all my clothes in the walk-in wardrobe with pink-and-white tiles and telling the joiners that the fewer shelves they gave me, the less crap I could put on them.

Jack was busy in his bedroom unpacking his shit in his typical boy's bedroom, which was all wooden and black.

My father was walking around the hallway at the bottom of the massive staircase with a fuck-off rifle bellowing, 'Sharon! Where shall I put this? Shall I put it under our bed?' The camera crew, who had put twenty-four fixed cameras around our house and set up a control room, were there capturing it all. It had been agreed that there would be no cameras in the bathrooms or toilets. A cameraman and sound guy would also be wandering around. Within the first hour of them being

'*Within the first hour*

of them being there,

my dad *decided he wanted to*

jump into the empty swimming pool

we were having built and

pretend to do breast-stroke.'

there, my dad decided he wanted to jump into the empty swimming pool we were having built and pretend to do breast-stroke.

The MTV guys were pissing themselves laughing at us all, but we were all kind of looking at them and then at each other thinking, 'Isn't this going to be a bit boring for the viewers?' There was no agenda. There wasn't some guy saying, 'Let's set this shit up, let's set that shit up.' They never told us what to do, they never scripted anything. So we were just getting on with our lives.

Jack was still at school, so Melinda dropped him off every morning. I should have been at Westmark too (the specialist school for kids with dyslexia) but I'd quit. It was a great school, but my mind was elsewhere. I just wasn't interested. There had been the initial talk about doing *The Osbournes* and my mind was on that and I didn't think I needed to finish my education.

Don't get me wrong. Walking out of school without completing my education wasn't the wisest thing I've ever done. I'm the first to admit that back then I wasn't clever or, rather, I wasn't academic. I worried every single day about what I was going to do with my life because I hated school so much and knew I wasn't doing well. Like everyone's parents, my mum and dad expected me to make my own money.

I T was the middle of the morning when I marched through the swinging kitchen doors and told my mum I wasn't ever going back to school. She wasn't particularly pleased. She was stood in the kitchen pretending to do something domesticated.

My mother can't cook. She simply can't cook. When my father was drinking, he used to hide his bottles of booze in the oven because he knew she wouldn't find them in there because she never opened the bloody oven door.

She said, 'If you're going to leave school, Kelly, you're going to have to be home-schooled.'

She brought in a tutor, but that lasted all of two weeks. Within three days I'd talked the tutor into doing all my work for me.

I thought I might like to work in the fashion industry or become a make-up artist. I'd grown up in a musical family, so working behind the scenes in the music world was also something I was considering. I had always been interested in how bands developed their image and brand.

My mum was adamant that I get a job if I was going to quit school and I was up for it. I started working in the office of a music management company, just off Robertson. I was literally starting at the bottom as the office girl, otherwise known as the coffee slut! I guess what my mum was trying to teach me was that just because you quit school you can't sit at home all day. I still had to get up and go to the office for 10 a.m. I'd make coffee, answer the phones, do the post and send faxes. I really enjoyed it. I got paid a hundred dollars a week. I learned so much and I wasn't at home sitting on my sorry arse. It also made me realise that sitting in a classroom just wasn't how I was going to learn. That first job taught me what it's like to be in an office environment. I had to be responsible and it taught me how to be disciplined. The only person who was going to get me to work in the morning was me.

The Osbournes

WHEN we started filming *The Osbournes*, I still worked at the music management company and for five months we just got on with our lives in front of the MTV crew. The novelty of wanting to look good for the cameras soon wore off. I stopped planning what I was going to wear the night before and even stopped bothering to put make-up on.

I was used to having a house full of people because it'd had been like that all my life. Our nanny Melinda was with us all the time, Uncle Tony had helped bring us up, there would be people coming to see my mum about Ozzfest and our housekeeper would always be about. Jack would have his friends hanging out in the house and I'd have mine over so it was constantly busy. Adding a camera crew to the mix really wasn't a big deal.

In 2002, the whole concept of 'reality TV' was in its infancy. There had never been anything like *The Osbournes* on television ever ever. It's since been described as the first reality-based comedy. In the UK there had been *Big Brother*, which started in 2000, the same year as the US version. But sticking a whole bunch of strangers into a house and watching them 24/7 was very different to what our show was about. For a start, my dad was already famous and the cameras were invited into our own home. But I think the biggest difference and the one that set us apart then – and still does today – is we were NEVER told what to do. We were simply living our lives. That's what made the show so unique. But because we were just getting on with what we'd always done as a family, it meant we didn't have any concept of how big it could get or how it would change our lives.

BIG Dave would also be hanging out with us. Can I just say, you have to use a deep voice when you say, 'Big Dave'. Deep voice, 'Big Dave'. He was our 'manny' and would be with us all the time. He used to be my dad's driver whenever he was working in New York. But during our visits to the Big Apple me, Jack and Aimee really hit it off with him too. Whenever Mum and Dad were working, he used to drive us around different places like the Statue of Liberty and Central Park. My mum saw how well he got on with us so she asked Big Dave if he'd consider moving to LA to keep an eye on us.

Big Dave rocks! He played a big part in my life during *The Osbournes* and when my dad goes on tour now, he still insists on Big Dave being with him.

At the beginning, I was aware of the cameras, of course. But it really didn't take long before I got used to them. That's why I didn't think it would change my life like it did. I'd be swinging in the Perspex chair hanging from the ceiling of my bedroom and I'd suddenly do a loud fart and think nothing of it – even though a fucking sound mike would be just millimetres away from my arse cheeks! That chair really made my farts echo.

Everything about my bedroom was fucking pink! I had pink walls and pink sofas, which were all different shapes – a bit like a jigsaw – and when you pieced them together they made one big sofa. I had white shutters at the window and matching white furniture. The cameras became part of the furniture too.

I suppose I was just going through the normal teenage stuff. Like one day, I decided to get a tattoo and talk about it on camera, but I still thought I would be able to keep it a secret from my mother. I didn't imagine they would show it on TV. I had also planned to keep it a secret from my father, but Big-mouth Jack told him.

I was sitting next to Dad on the flowery sofa in the kitchen while Jack sat in the chair. We were all watching the Discovery Channel (my dad fucking loves it, and the History Channel, they're his favourites) on the flat screen attached to the wall when Jack managed to purposely let slip that I'd had a tattoo.

My dad jumped up and said, 'What's this all about then Kelly? Have you had a fucking tattoo? Have you? You've got to be careful, man!? I had one that went septic on my arm.'

So, in the end, I was forced to show him the tiny red heart I'd had tattooed on my hip bone. But only on condition he didn't tell Mum. Straight away he was on the phone to Mum in the hairdresser's telling her as she had her hair washed at the sink.

I could hear him on the phone saying, 'It's actually not that bad, Sharon.'

When I went to meet her from the hairdresser's she said, 'Well, let's see it then.'

The damage was done, what could she do? That's the great thing about tattoos; you can't have them removed when your parents go mad . . . but that's the problem too.

Fierce

I now have sixteen tattoos and I hate them. There is no story behind my tattoos apart from stupidity! Well, actually, there are some stories, like I got 'Daddy' written on my forearm when my dad had his quad bike accident. I went with Jack on his eighteenth birthday to get his first tattoo. He got my name on his wrist and I got his. I've got my mum's name on my back. The last tattoo I got was 'Lovely' written on my wrist and my boyfriend Luke got the same (it's our nickname for each other).

I do think getting a tattoo is a form of self-harm because it hurts and it's not fun; it's a control thing. Already I'm looking into how to get rid of them. What I liked when I was sixteen was not what I liked when I was seventeen and it was definitely not what I liked when I was eighteen. If only I had waited when I decided I wanted a tattoo – I wouldn't have half of them now.

My dad's tattoos all represent a different time in his life and they seem to have more of a story than a random dolphin jumping out of the sea plastered on your ankle. At least I didn't have one of those.

T HEN there was the time I decided to get my nose pierced. I'd pre-warned my mum I was thinking about it and straight away she told me not to do it. But I waited until I'd gone away with friends for the weekend and came back and presented it to my mum. She was messing around doing something in the games room, standing in front of the snooker table next to the juke box. I stood there in a black hooded top and khaki trousers waiting for my mum to notice the tiny stud in my nose.

And sure enough she did. Her first words were, 'Have you had your nose pierced, Kelly? It looks like a bogey. Please take it out.'

I was trying not to laugh because there was nothing she could do about it. But she carried on, 'Kelly, you are going to be heartbroken that you have a big hole in your nose when you get older. You will regret having that in your face.'

THE night before the first episode of *The Osbournes* was due to air, me, Mum and Jack went for a walk with the dogs on Venice Beach in Santa Monica. My mum was really nervous and she said to us, 'Why did we agree to do the show? People are going to think we're so stupid.'

Jack and I agreed with her. We were all genuinely shitting ourselves and were convinced that we had made the biggest mistake of our lives.

The next night we all piled into my dad's room, which we called The Bunker, to watch the first episode on MTV. It was where Dad did all his music, painting (my dad is a fucking good artist) and writing. There was me, Jack, Mum and Dad, a couple of executives from MTV, our nanny Melinda, *deep voice* Big Dave and everyone from Mum's office.

And the theme music came on (a cover of one of my dad's hits 'Crazy Train') 'Crazy, but that's how it goes . . .' and straight away I had to put my hand over my face and just peer at the screen from behind the gaps between my fingers. I hated seeing myself on screen. I hated the way I looked. I hated my voice, my pink hair, the way I dressed – everything! The other

Fierce

surprise was that Jack and I were on screen a fucking lot! We had not expected it. Of course, we pissed ourselves laughing when they showed my dad going mental because he couldn't use the remote control to the television. It was just typical of my dad, who was always shouting for Jack to come and help him work it out so he wouldn't be forced to watch the weather channel all fucking day.

The half-hour episode went so quickly and at the end we all just breathed a sigh of relief that we'd got through it and had managed not to look too ridiculous. We also thought hardly anyone would have watched it.

I hated seeing myself on screen.

I hated the way I looked.

I hated my voice, my pink hair,

the way I dressed – everything!

The next day, I was driving on my own along Sunset when I looked in my rear-view mirror and saw I was being followed by another car. It didn't matter which side street I turned off on, the car was behind me. I just froze. My heart was pounding. I kept one hand on the wheel and with the other I scrambled in my bag on the front passenger seat for my mobile phone. I called Big Dave and blurted out in a panic, 'Dave, someone's following me. I'm so scared.'

I pulled into a parking space along Sunset while I waited for him to come and find me. He was only minutes away and was laughing his head off as he walked towards my car. As he peered his head into the window of my car, he said, 'Kelly, they're photographers.' Wham! I thought, 'Fuck, my life is never going to be the same again.' But I couldn't understand why they would want to take a picture of me. I really couldn't.

The fame, if you can call it that, was instant. During the first week after the show had gone out, I would open the white shutters in my bedroom and see the whole street full of cars with paparazzi sitting inside with their cameras resting on their opened windows. Or they'd be huddled at the entrance of the gates, waiting to pounce whenever one of us drove out. They were there twenty-four hours a day.

The other freaky thing that started to happen was strangers would come and just hang outside our house. They were obviously fans of the show, but at the time it didn't register with me. I just couldn't get my head around why someone would want to sit on the pavement outside the house of a bunch of people they'd never met.

I wasn't stupid. I was more than aware of what a fan was. I'd grown up with a father who had millions of them, but he'd been famous since he was nineteen and was a talented musician.

We'd let the cameras into our home for one night and all of a sudden people were camping outside.

I came down the stairs one afternoon and there were two girls standing in our hallway. So I smiled and said 'hi' and walked into the kitchen. My dad was standing at the sink looking out into the garden and I said, 'Dad, who are those girls in our house?'

He turned around and said, 'Aren't they mates of yours, Kelly? They rang the buzzer on the gate so I let them in.'

I replied, 'No, Dad. I've never fucking seen them before in my life.'

They were complete strangers who'd just watched the show and rocked up outside. I was bent double pissing myself laughing. My dad shot past me and started shouting, 'What the fuck are you doing in my house? Get out of my house.'

It was the funniest thing ever!

AFTER the show, Jack and I would walk into a shop and everyone would just stop what they were doing and stare at us like we were aliens or something. Los Angeles is full of A-list celebrities, so we thought it was so strange that people would give a shit about two teenagers. I found the whole thing really confusing.

Jack and I were already known at places like The Roxy and The Standard Hotel, but all of a sudden we didn't have to queue up outside. We'd always been able to walk straight into On The Rox but we never got preferential treatment at the other clubs. Sometimes we didn't even get in.

But that first time we went out after the first episode had aired was so surreal. As we walked up to The Roxy, the guys on the door just ushered us to the front and we went straight in. Now, I'm not going to lie; not having to queue up was the coolest thing ever and, yeah, we fucking loved it. Who wouldn't? Once we were inside, Jack just turned to me and said, 'What the fuck? Did that just happen?'

But it did start to freak us out after a while. When people are being so kind to you all the time, you do wonder what they want.

Quite possibly the most random thing that happened was that people started offering me cocaine. I'd be out and some random guy would come straight over to me and say, 'Do you want to buy some coke?' Or they would give me their card and say, 'If you ever want to score any drugs, give me a call.' I was seventeen. These dealers obviously thought that if you were famous and you have money, you could become an addict and then make them lots of money. It was quite unbelievable. Of course I wasn't naïve about drugs – I was regularly taking painkillers, for fuck's sake – but I didn't associate that kind of addiction to cocaine use at that point.

I wasn't naïve either to the fact that people offered drugs, but it was usually less blatant and mostly when they had taken something themselves and wanted to share. These guys were stone-cold sober and on a mission to find new customers. I

144

would always say no and walk away. I had grown up with a father who took drugs, but that didn't mean that I had thought about taking cocaine myself. Now that I was famous, did people really think I would be interested?

The first time anyone asked for my autograph was just crazy. Had I practised before? Had I fuck! My father was due at an album signing at a record store on Sunset and me, Melinda, Big Dave and my uncle Tony had gone ahead of my mum and dad who were arriving in a black stretch limousine, much to my dad's annoyance because he hates them.

There was a roped-off area in front of a curtain partially dividing the fans lining the streets in front of the red carpet. We were all standing behind the curtain waiting for my dad to arrive. I popped my head around the curtain to see if my dad was there and someone shouted, 'Kelly! It's Kelly Osbourne.'

And then the entire crowd started chanting, 'Kelly! Kelly! Kelly!'

Hearing my name was just so weird. Our nanny, Melinda, pushed me forward to have my picture taken and sign autographs. My whole body was squirming with embarrassment. People started touching me and grabbing my coat. It was one of the oddest experiences of my life.

WE were asked to do some really crazy shit during the first series of *The Osbournes*. Here's an indication of what everyone thought of me: I was approached to do anything associated with being fat or weight loss. Production companies wanted me to stop eating, continue eating, interview fat people, thin people, visit the fattest cities in America – all kinds of shit. I didn't want to do any of them. But hey, I'd got the message: everyone thought I was fat.

The best request that came through was one that Jack got. He was asked to go into the jungle and purposely get bitten by all the most poisonous snakes and spiders in the world to see what it felt like. But he didn't need to worry because the production company was going to give him an antidote to take straight after so he wouldn't die. That's if it worked, of course. I'm not being funny, but why the fuck would he want to do that? Go out and try and get killed, oh and just for the fun of it, invite a TV crew along as well. Idiots!

THERE were so many things that made me proud of the show. Amongst all the craziness I wanted people to see we were a real family with the same family values as everyone else. Before that show, everyone thought my father lived in some fucking bat cave. Nothing made me prouder than when my father finally got a star on the Hollywood Walk of Fame in Los Angeles. It had been set up way before the show, but because we were now being followed by the MTV crew, they came too.

The Hollywood Walk of Fame is a tribute to stars past and present and it's such a big honour to have your name on a star embedded in the sidewalk. Destiny's Child, Matt Damon, Whoopi Goldberg. Frank Sinatra . . . it's a really big deal. My mum had been trying for ages to get my dad on the Hollywood Walk of Fame because he deserved it. When it comes to music, he created a whole genre of music with Black Sabbath and again when he went solo.

Fierce

So many people look to him for inspiration. One morning my mum finally got a letter in the post to say that my dad would be getting a star. I was so fucking proud, I can't tell you.

But there was a problem; my mum wanted us to keep it a secret from him as long as possible. He had been invited to unveil his star (every star has to be there at the unveiling or they don't get one – unless they're dead) on 12 April 2002. In the end he was the only person who didn't know and it was killing us not to tell him. About three weeks before, my mum took him into the kitchen and we all waited outside and she said, 'Ozzy, you're going to get a star on the Hollywood Walk of Fame.'

He said, 'Are you kidding, Sharon?'

We all burst in and my mum was squealing, 'No, Daddy (it's what she always calls my dad.) I'm not joking.'

We were all jumping around him – it was brilliant.

When the day arrived it was bloody stressful because we were all so nervous for him. My half-brother and -sister Louis and Jessica had flown over and there was my mum, me, Jack, Aimee, Uncle Tony, Melinda and Lynn Seager, who has been my mum's best friend for ever and runs her management company in the UK. We all had to be there for 11.30 a.m. As we pulled into Hollywood Boulevard there were literally thousands of people waiting on the pavement to see my dad. I had goose bumps all over my body as we stepped out of the car. I don't think I've ever felt more proud in my whole life.

My father stepped out and said, 'This is just so overwhelming with all of you turning out so early in the morning to see my old butt.' It was an amazing day.

CHAPTER TEN

EATING MY FEELINGS

What struck me was that the magazines were not just criticising me, they were also labelling any other girl in the world who was the same size as me.

WHEN *The Osbournes* show started, I knew I wasn't skinny, but I just thought I was normal. I was a UK size ten (American size six) and I was 5ft 2in. I'm short, so of course I'm going to look that bit bigger than someone who is 5ft 4in and a size ten. But I would never have considered myself as fat. I really wasn't prepared for the whole world to have an opinion on my appearance.

The first time I read that people thought I was fat was in *US Weekly*, a gossip magazine in America. It was the issue that had come out the week after the first episode of *The Osbournes*.

I was flicking through it while sitting on the sofa in the kitchen at Doheny. It was exciting to see myself in a magazine that I'd been reading for years. We were all still very surprised at how well received that first show had been, so everything felt new and fun.

But when I read the words that went with the piece, I couldn't believe it. I forget the exact details of the article. I just read FAT. It felt like someone was crushing my heart. It was that overwhelming. I got this hot feeling that made me feel like my face was on fire. It was sheer panic and sadness. I burst into tears. I kept thinking, 'How can you think this?' I was practically a child. It destroyed me. It really did. I just wasn't prepared for that level of criticism.

I was sat there, curled up on the sofa in my own home, where I had always felt so safe and happy. All of a sudden, it felt like I was public property and there was nothing I could do. Where do you hide? It was there in black and white for everyone to read. From that moment on, I saw life as Before *The Osbournes* and After *The Osbournes*. Those references to me being fat also really upset my mum too. She does this thing where she puts a shit in a box and sends it to someone who has upset us. She used to get Jack to shit in a box when he was a baby too. Really normal parenting, yeah? Obviously, Mum would do this to someone who had said something about her family. My mum always says that you can say whatever you want about her, but don't slag off her husband or her children. She used to place the shit in one of those lovely blue boxes from the upmarket jewellers Tiffany's. The she would send it to whoever had pissed her off. She hasn't done it for a while, though people still think that she does it.

When the show came out, there was one guy who wrote a review of *The Osbournes* in a well-respected newspaper. He made reference to the kids being fat. Mum thought that article

'Don't get me wrong,

it was really upsetting what they'd written.

Jack and I were just kids.

But she can't fight our battles.

She really can't.'

was really irresponsible. So she got someone to shit in a box and sent it to him with a note saying, 'I've heard you've got an eating disorder? Eat this.'

Can I just say, my mum has got to stop fighting my battles for me! I mean, when she sent that shit to the journalist from the newspaper, well, that was just plain crazy. Don't get me wrong, it was really upsetting what they'd written. Jack and I were just kids. But she can't fight our battles. She really can't.

I consoled myself with one fact: you could bet your life that the person who wrote that article would have been one ugly motherfucker!

When we started filming *The Osbournes* in the October, I was still taking a Vicodin when I went out, but nothing more than one or two at the weekend. In the same way that people get drunk at a weekend, I'd take a Vicodin. I'd drink too, but never to excess.

When the *The Osbournes* aired on 5 March 2002, I'd started taking maybe one or two pills during the week. I'd begun to build up a bit of a resistance and so I was taking two tablets to get the same feeling I'd experienced that very first night. I was aware that other people I was hanging out with were also taking them, but for me it wasn't a communal thing. Apart from the guy I was buying them from, who was now a friend, no one else really knew. My parents certainly didn't have a clue.

But I began to rely on Vicodin more and more to help me cope with the downsides of fame. Not knowing how to deal with it meant any articles making reference to my size really got to me. I think I was always someone who was going to have weight issues, but I don't think it would have been such a big problem had I not become famous.

I started to binge-eat – big time. It was the start of a vicious circle. Publications would call me fat and it would really hurt my feelings. So then I would comfort-eat to make myself feel better.

Was I fat? Of course I wasn't. But it didn't matter by then because I'd convinced myself that I was. I went up to a UK size fourteen and I was so miserable and hated myself and didn't care what I looked like and didn't put any effort into what I wore.

When I say binge, I wasn't one of those people who wouldn't eat for ages and then all of a sudden would eat a million burgers and then make themselves puke. It was more a case of eating to comfort myself, which meant I'd turn to quick fixes – junk food. I was eating too much bad stuff. I used to eat everything I could get my hands on. I was miserable. I was eating my feelings. I was eating tons of crisps.

I was only seventeen and so unbelievably sensitive. There is nothing wrong with that. Everyone is at that age. What you want to hear is positive things about yourself. What you don't need to hear is loads of people saying you're fat. I would eat to make myself feel better. Crisps, chips, chocolate, sweets . . . I didn't feel guilty afterwards, no. But I did get fatter, which made me feel even more fucking miserable.

I needed food and quickly. I wasn't interested in cooking anything. I would just grab whatever was available. I was also drinking endless cans of fizzy drinks – they're my big downfall.

Eating My Feelings

There is so much sugar and calories in those drinks. French fries from McDonald's were also a big favourite of mine. I would jump in my car and drive to the nearby restaurant and buy the largest box and eat them straight away. Then sometimes I'd go back and buy another box.

Jack was also suffering from a similar problem. There was one time I visited a burger joint I'd not normally go to, but that Jack would go to all the time. I refused to go because on the television advert for the restaurant, when the man took a bite out of a burger it made a horrible chewing sound that went right through me. People chewing noisily – gum, crisps, crackers, whatever – is my biggest pet hate. Friends do it to wind me up now. They'll put the biggest piece of chewing gum in their mouth and then chew it really loudly in my ear. Fuck, it drives me absolutely insane. It really does.

But that night my friend really wanted to go to the burger joint I hated, so I went with her. When I walked through the door they just assumed that I was collecting my brother's 'usual'. It dawned on me that my brother was also binge eating.

I think weight gain is caused by a mixture of things; genetics definitely play a part. I think Jack and I will always struggle with our weight to some extent. My mum has a problem with her weight too. But I also think it's about how you deal with big situations in your life. I eat when I'm stressed out, I eat when I'm not stressed. I'm just one of those people who turn to food no matter what. As I've got older, I've learned to recognise the signs. But the truth is, it doesn't matter if you put weight on. Of course, it's not good for your health to be obese. But I think –

especially if you're a woman – that your weight is going to yo-yo. That's perfectly normal.

I've been thin – a UK size six – and I've been bigger – oh my God, shock horror I've been a size fourteen – but should it really matter? One of the times when I was a UK fourteen I'd just come out of rehab when I was twenty-one. I was trying to win my battle with drug addiction and I'd just moved to start a new life. It was probably the first time I really wasn't bothered about my weight, it was the least of my worries.

When I was in the musical *Chicago* in the West End, I started to lose weight. I was in a routine and I felt happy. I usually lose weight when I'm feeling settled and content. Or I'm doing so much stuff my mind is distracted from food. I was incredibly busy juggling the theatre production with my Radio 1 show as well as doing press and publicity.

The funny thing is, even when I've been at my biggest, I've never felt self-conscious if I've been pictured next to someone really skinny. It's a good fucking job!

What I've learned through the media is that they look down on someone for being fat far more than for being a junkie. Magazines see it as such a massive crime. It really is quite unbelievable.

During those first few weeks of *The Osbournes* I was referred to as 'fat, big, overweight . . .' and the list goes on. It doesn't matter what size I am physically; I'm a fat person in my head – because everyone still tells me I am.

Even when I've lost weight, magazines and newspapers have still written that I'm fat or they say that I've 'ditched the diet'

Eating My Feelings

when I've put on two pounds. They love to publish pictures of me that compare when I was thinner and then fatter. Like, what the fuck? Every time they write that shit I think to myself, 'Oh come on. I've done far more shitty things that you could write about.'

The thing that struck me as well was that the magazines were not just criticising me, they were also labelling as fat any other girl in the world who was the same size as me.

How fucked up is that?

At the beginning, my battle with my weight would probably have been fine if I could have hidden away. But *The Osbournes* was attracting massive viewing figures which meant that we had started on this huge merry-go-round of press and publicity.

I LEARNED very early on that I was never going to be one of those people who hugely posed on the red carpet. The day my dad got his star on the Hollywood Walk of Fame was the first time I'd been to an event where there were loads of photographers interested in taking my picture. When we were at that event, we were being bombarded. Uncle Tony turned to us and said, 'This is something else. I've never seen anything like this.'

He'd spent years with my dad and witnessed how Dad would always get mobbed by masses of fans. But even he was blown away by the sheer numbers, including journalists and photographers who had turned up. It was less than a month after that first episode of *The Osbournes*. It was completely insane.

On that morning in Hollywood, I didn't have a fucking clue what to do. I just stood there frozen to the spot. No one suddenly

'*No one **suddenly***

appears

*out of nowhere **when you***

find fame and starts

to teach you what to do.'

Eating My Feelings

appears out of nowhere when you find fame and starts to teach you what to do. Maybe in years to come, there will be a special 'What to do when you get famous' school.

The flashes from the cameras were going crazy, they were practically blinding me. I didn't know where to look or what to do with my body or hands or anything! A TV reporter stuck a camera in front of my face and I just talked. About what, I couldn't fucking tell you. No one had prepared me for the instant fame.

Mum's best friend Lynn was with me and she was brimming with tears. She told me afterwards that she'd felt so proud of me. But I didn't really know what I'd done. I'd just talked, which is something I'm very good at.

If you notice, in pictures (I still do it today) I always look like I've just smelt a shit because I've got this expression I do when I'm really nervous. I sort of move my nostrils in a funny way. Whenever I've looked at other people on the red carpet they're really going for it. They stick their arses out. Then they look over their shoulder and give a cheeky grin. Who teaches them how to do that shit? I could never be like that. I don't want to be like that. The most I can do is put my hand on my hip.

Because I was binge-eating, I'd put on some weight, which just made me feel even more self-conscious. I couldn't tell you how much, but my clothes felt a bit tighter. I was not big by any means, but I was miserable. I'd started to hate the way I looked.

I don't agree with faddy diets. I never have and I never will. When I was at school I was the one person who was never on some crazy diet. There would be girls who were only eating fruit or following some fad diet where they were only allowed liquids. But to some extent, I think trying different diets is a part of growing up.

But having seen my mum suffer so much with weight over the years had made me never want to go on a diet. I just wasn't interested in following some crazy plan where I only ate vegetables before noon or something else equally fucking ridiculous!

My mum has been bulimic and anorexic. For years she yo-yo dieted. She has done every diet you can think of: Slim Fast, where you only drink shakes and then one 'regular meal' per day; Atkins, where you don't eat carbohydrates. There was another one where she would only do milkshakes. Then she went through a phase where someone would deliver food to our house. They were all short-term solutions that didn't deal with a bigger issue. As a kid, seeing her suffer bothered me. I didn't want my mum to be unhappy. But seeing her go through all that made me promise myself that I would never put myself in the same situation.

Before we started doing *The Osbournes*, my mum had heard of an operation you could have that effectively made an overweight person's stomach smaller to stop their intake of food and help them get thinner. She was desperate to do it – she was effectively agreeing to be a guinea pig.

She sat me, Dad, Jack and Aimee down one evening and explained to us that she was going to get a gastric band. Actually, first she was going to get the one where they actually cut your stomach and make it smaller. It's the gastric bypass.

But when she went to see the specialist and they said that she would have to fill out a form saying that if she died it wasn't their fault, she decided not to do it.

So then she did some more investigating and put herself forward to be the test dummy for the band. And we were all, as any children would be, scared and worried about it. She invited the doctor to our house in LA and we all sat together and discussed it. We understood it, because the doctor explained it really well. Part of us didn't want her to do it but we wanted her to be happy, so we said she should do it.

On the morning of the operation, my dad went with her to the hospital, Cedars-Sinai. She didn't want me, Jack or Aimee to go with her.

Within weeks, she started to lose the weight really quickly and it made her really happy and it changed things a lot. I always say that my mum is the centre of our family and people react to her. So if she is in a bad mood, it pisses off my dad and then us, and before you know it, we're all in a bad mood. And it works in the same way when she is happy. Well, losing all this weight made her really happy, so that was good for us too.

MY mum is addicted to having plastic surgery. She really is. I hate it when she gets work done. I always have.

She has got this miraculous way of saying to us, 'Oh, I am just going in for a routine operation.' There is nothing fucking routine about getting your tits done, Mum!

My mum and Botox – seriously! When she used to be bulimic she would leave the table after dinner to go and throw up. We

Fierce

'

She has got this miraculous way of

saying to us,

"Oh, I am just going in

for a routine operation."

There is nothing fucking routine about

getting your tits done, Mum!

'

knew what she was up to. We didn't like it, but there was nothing we could do about it. But the thing that used to really annoy us was that she'd come back and have blood all over her forehead from where her Botox injections had strained as she'd been sick. And she'd still deny it. We'd say, 'Mum, you've had Botox again.'

She would reply, 'No I didn't.'

'Yes you did – your head is fucking bleeding,' we'd all say in unison.

Gay cousin Terry had a friend who did fillers and Botox at your home. During a visit to see one of my aunties in Birmingham, my mum decided to have her lips plumped. I am not joking; you know when you see shows on TV about surgery disasters? She could have appeared on one of those. She looked like one of those babies whose parents buy them a dummy with big lips painted on the outside so it looks like the baby has big lips. She looked just like that. My dad's sisters could not stop laughing.

Later that day, we travelled to see Mum's friend Elton John at his home in London. We were all sitting around his dining room table. He did really well, but then he just couldn't keep it to himself. He said, 'Sharon, what the fuck has happened to your lips?' We all just burst out laughing. He sent her to a doctor to get it fixed.

I'm forever turning to my mum and saying to her, 'What's wrong, mum? You look like you've seen a ghost.'

Her eyebrows will be raised and she'll have a look of shock on her face. She'll say 'No Kelly, the botox went wrong again.'

I will have plastic surgery one day, simply because I don't want to get saggy. I don't want droopy tits or one of those

Fierce

horrible chicken chins. You know when someone has too much fat hanging from under their chin and you can sort of flick it?

Now, I wouldn't even think of it. It would hurt too much and what if it messed up? No, I'm not ready for any of that yet.

My mum hasn't put me off some surgery, but she has opened my eyes to it. I think my mum has been incredibly lucky with her surgery. She does look amazing. But if she doesn't stop she is going to look like cat woman, I kid you not! It's an addiction – one hundred per cent.

CHAPTER ELEVEN

TRYING TO BE STRONG

'Kelly, mum's got cancer.'

AFTER the first season of *The Osbournes*, we were approached to do an album of our favourite songs. I thought it was a cool idea, but I really didn't think anything more about it. It was just something my mum was sorting out.

Then my mum came up with this idea that Aimee would sing one of the songs on the album. Aimee didn't want to do it, so she suggested I did it. The Madonna song 'Papa Don't Preach' was picked out. It was my mum's idea and somehow I got involved in singing it.

There was a selection of songs on *The Osbourne Family Album* like 'Dreamer' by my dad, 'Drive' by The Cars, 'You Really Got Me' by The Kinks, 'Imagine' by John Lennon and a whole bunch of other songs.

I went to a studio in Venice, which is a district in western Los Angeles, to record the single. Venice is known for its beaches and has vendors and performers along the front. I met up with a couple of guys from an American band called Incubus, who were going to help produce it. It was so weird because even though I had been in the studio loads of times with my dad, I was so fucking nervous. I'd always been on the other side – I'd never stood there with the headphones on. People find it strange when I say that the whole recording process was new to me. But it really was. I mean, if my father had been a welder I wouldn't have instantly been able to pick up a torch and known how to use it, would I?

I wasn't taking myself too seriously on that first day. I wasn't standing there wearing my earphone over one ear and the other resting on my cheek like I'd seen so many other recording artists do thinking, 'Hey, I'm going to be the next big thing in pop music.'

It was fun. It was bullshit. I opened my mouth, I could sing, it seemed, and it went on to the album. And then it very quickly became really real and to me that was a whole different ball game . . .

After *The Family Album* came out and people heard my version of Madonna's song, I got offered a million dollars for a record deal from Epic Records. I thought, I don't give a shit about this, but I would be so fucking stupid if I didn't take that money.

I co-wrote a few of the songs with the team. This is the thing I can't stand about a lot of artists today. They say they write everything by themselves – they fucking don't. They don't do that. Most songs are co-written. At least I'm honest enough to admit it.

THE plan was that I was going to record the album in New York so Mum, Jack, Aimee and Melinda flew with me from Los Angeles to help me settle in.

We'd agreed to do a second season of *The Osbournes* following the success of the first one, so we had the MTV crew with us when we flew to New York. We'd got so used to the camera crew being around that we didn't even notice they were there half the time.

We all arrived at the apartment in Trump Towers, where I was going to stay during the six weeks of recording. Mum and Melinda spent the day helping me settle in and buying groceries.

That evening we all had our own plans. I was going for dinner with Nicole Richie at the Japanese restaurant Nobu. Nicole and I had become friends after our initial introduction years earlier at The Standard Hotel on Sunset in LA.

I was sitting in the restaurant when my mobile started ringing. It was Jack and he was crying, saying, 'Kelly, you have to come back to the hotel.'

I wasn't in the mood for it, so I said, 'Jack, if you just had a fight with Mum, I'm not coming back.'

He answered back, 'No! We need you to come back.'

I really thought he was being dramatic and was screaming back in the middle of the crowded restaurant, 'Come on, Jack. Stop messing me about here.'

He just sobbed, 'Kelly, Mum's got cancer.'

Trying To Be Strong

I mean, I just fucking lost it. I practically fell to the floor in the middle of the restaurant. Nicole had to pick me up. I was crying so much. I've never cried like that before. She was holding me up and guiding me to a taxi waiting outside. My mascara was all over her white dress from my streaming black face. I was a mess. I was in pieces. She put me in the taxi and I flopped my head against the window and I just sobbed uncontrollably. It was about a block away, but I couldn't get there quick enough. I really couldn't. It felt like the longest journey ever.

I ran into the hotel and up to the room and found mum. She was sitting on the floor in one of the rooms with her legs crossed like she always does. She looked in shock. Really, really shocked. We all did. I just held her. I couldn't hold her tight enough. That evening she'd received a call from at her office in LA. They had been faxed the results of a medical Mum had had recently. She had been diagnosed with colon cancer.

Straightaway, we all started grabbing our stuff and we literally fled the hotel. I think we had just a small bag each. We really weren't thinking – we just wanted to get home to my dad. We wanted Mum to start her treatment straight away.

The office had organised a private jet for us so we could get straight back to LA. On the plane we were all clinging on to each other. None of us wanted to let go of Mum. I was holding on to her for dear life. I just couldn't comprehend what was happening. We were all shit scared.

My dad and Uncle Tony met us from the plane in like a golf buggy. Mum had called Dad from New York. When we finally walked into the house he just broke down.

Fierce

‘ *I ran into the hotel and up to the room and found mum.* She was sitting on the floor in one of the rooms *with her legs crossed like she always does. She looked in shock.*

Really, really shocked.

We all did. ’

Mum went straight into hospital for treatment. We all dealt with the news so differently. Jack went completely off the rails. He hardly ever visited Mum in hospital – he's terrified of them. He just went out and got high. My dad lost it big time. He just drank and drank and drank and drank. I totally understand why he did. He thought the love of his life was going to die.

Aimee turned into a mother figure and was bossing us all around. She was doing what she thought was best, but sometimes she came across as too harsh.

I just didn't want to let my mum out of my sight, so I moved into the hospital. She went into Cedars-Sinai for treatment. I put my plans to record the album on hold for a short while and stayed with her. I slept on the floor on a roll-up bed.

I was trying to be strong for my mum, so I was taking Vicodin to hide the pain. I didn't want to leave her side for one minute. I also wanted to numb the terrible sadness I was feeling.

My friends would try and persuade me to go out with them but every time I did, I'd be sitting in The Roxy or The Standard Hotel wondering how my mum was and whether she would be OK. Or there would be other times when I would get completely wasted so I didn't have to think about it. And then I would go home and not back to the hospital because I didn't want my mum to see me in that state.

I'm not going to lie, it was a really terrible time. I'm embarrassed to admit it now, but in my head I often thought I'd kill myself if my mum didn't make it. I thought, if Mum dies, that will be it. I wouldn't be able to cope without Mum. She was, and is, the centre of our universe.

Fierce

I knew that Dad would kill himself if anything happened to Mum because he wouldn't be able to take it. I couldn't take it. But I had to be strong for Mum and not think of such stupid things like I would kill myself. Mum needed me.

I swear to God, Mum just carried on working while she was in hospital getting her treatment – she never stopped. She didn't want to admit to herself that she was sick. I think that's probably what got her through – it stopped her focussing on just how ill she was. My mum's a fighter.

She insisted that the MTV crew continued filming the second series of the show because she wanted everything to be as normal as possible. She was putting on a brave face for us. I knew she was.

My mum is the person we all go to when we have a problem – my dad, me, my brother and sister – everyone. She's always so strong. But who does my mum go to when she needs to talk to someone? That worried me so much. Of course she has friends – Lynn, who runs the UK office, is her best friend and she could always talk to her. But Mum usually tries to stay strong for everyone.

There was a time when my mum started to lose her hair because of the chemotherapy she was having. That was really tough. My mum's hair is her signature feature. It's thick and lovely. That was when she thought she was going to die.

She wrote a wish list of all the things she wanted to do before she died and she put her make-up artist Jude in charge of the plans. One of them was that she wanted her and my dad to renew their wedding vows. The ceremony took place on New

Trying To Be Strong

Year's Eve, 2002 – five months after she was first diagnosed with cancer – at the Beverly Hills Hotel.

I can't even bear to look at that video now. I just can't look at it. It makes me so sad. It was around this time we got Cher's wig-maker to make my mum's wigs. To cheer Mum up we used to put them on the dogs at home and take pictures. When she was asleep we'd frame them and leave them on the bedside table to make her laugh when she woke up.

Do you know just how cruel some people were when they heard my mum had cancer? One woman actually faxed my mum's office in LA and accused her of pulling a publicity stunt. How fucked up is that? Someone else emailed and said, 'Sharon, you've pulled some publicity stunts in your time, but this . . .' I couldn't believe it.

Our nanny Melinda was so fantastic around this time. She was instrumental in keeping our family together and for that I'll always be really grateful. She looked out for all of us.

MUM was adamant that I continue with the album and so I started to go back into the recording studio. At first it felt like an adventure. I got to play around in the recording studio. But all of that changed very quickly. The novelty wore off. On top of worrying about my mum, I felt like a lot was being asked of me and I was too young to deal with it. I really cracked under all the responsibility and pressure. I felt like I was tied to the music and I just wasn't passionate enough about it to not care about the other

'It was around this time we got Cher's

wig-maker to make my mum's wigs.

To cheer mum up we used to put them

on the dogs at home and take pictures.

When she was asleep we'd frame them and

leave them on the bedside table

to make her laugh when she woke up. '

things that were happening in my life at that time.

I was so miserable. I was recording an album – it should have been one of the most fun things to do, but my mind wasn't there. It was my mum's idea to call my first album *Shut Up*. The second single was called that, too. I didn't like the name and I didn't want to call it that. Hearing that song in my head now makes me shudder and go, 'Urgh!'

I'm not ashamed of it in any way, but my God it's a harsh reflection, put it that way. In the video, I had a really blunt bob with a fringe and was running around a recording studio with my band in the background! Oh my God, I'm so embarrassed! I was skidding around on my knees on the floor and generally just dicking around and slamming my microphone on the floor. Oh and then I ate the head off a chocolate bat or something. Of course I knew I was lucky to get an album, but I'm sure some people will be surprised to hear that I really didn't think that much of it. It was given to me. Half of me thought, 'These people are really fucking stupid for thinking that just because the show is popular people are going to buy my album. And then the other half of me was thinking, 'I might become the biggest pop star in the world.'

The first time I performed live was at the MTV Movie Awards in June 2002 at the Shrine Auditorium in Los Angeles. I was singing 'Papa Don't Preach'. I ran down the stairs and on to the stage. My mum, who was still very sick and so terribly frail, was in the audience with the people from her office. Jack was recording it and was running around all over the place with a hand-held video camera.

Fierce

It was the first time Mum had ever seen me perform in front of a live audience and her face was a picture. She had her hands over her mouth in excitement – and nerves, probably.

I'd dyed half of my hair bright pink and the other half was black. At the time I thought I looked so cool; I was wearing a bright pink shirt and a black blazer. I just jumped around a lot. I was nervous. But really what was going through my head was, 'OK, you can do this. The song is three-and-a-half minutes. In three-and-a-half minutes you'll be able to take pills and you won't be able to remember if you fuck up anyway.' I wouldn't have dreamed of taking any painkillers before I went on stage. Not then, anyway.

By then, I'd come to rely on taking painkillers to get me through difficult times or numb a feeling I didn't want to have.

When I jumped on to the stage I was excited and there was a part of me that thought, 'This is fucking amazing.' But then I looked out at the audience of A-list celebrities sitting on the front row staring back at me. I kept thinking 'You'll never be as good as them, you'll never be as skinny as them . . . There was Ben Affleck, Vin Diesel and Natalie Portman – a whole bunch of big names.

It's so crazy how I'm really confident in some ways, but in other ways I feel so insecure. Maybe that's why I didn't cope with my singing career very well.

Shut Up came out in November 2006 and debuted at number one on *Billboard*'s 'Heatseekers' chart in America – that was pretty cool. I felt proud, but I still wasn't happy. Of course there were the usual people slagging it off.

Trying To Be Strong

'It's so crazy how *I'm really confident* in some ways, but in other ways *I feel so insecure*. Maybe that's why I didn't cope with my singing career very well.'

Soon after, I left Epic and signed with Sanctuary. I recorded my second album, *Sleeping in the Nothing*, which came out in 2005. It was less pop punk and more eighties and I loved it. 'One Word' was the first song released. It could have done better than the first one but I fucked it up. I was stupid. I wasn't sticking to obligations or commitments. I didn't honour my commitment and that was foolish. I was letting myself down in every way I could. Maybe if I'd put more into it, it could have done better. A lot of people have come up to me since and said how much they liked that album, so that's good. I liked it too. But I just didn't realise how much I liked it at the time.

The record companies had a set idea of what they wanted me to be like and at the time of my first album, the singer Avril Lavigne was huge. Because I came from the 'rock scene' I was expected to have a similar image, but it really wasn't me. They wanted me to be the girl who rocked out and gave the middle finger. I wanted to be more of a pop person – I wanted to be more like the Disney stars who came out and sang pop songs. They always looked like they were having lots of fun. I should have turned around and said I was unhappy with the image they wanted me to have, but I didn't.

Of course I love my dad and appreciate his music, but I was the biggest pop-music fan ever – I still am. I loved New Kids on the Block, Bananarama and the Backstreet Boys. I was also the biggest Pet Shop Boys fan – I used to call them the Ketchup Boys. Whenever their music videos came on TV I would watch them.

The one thing in England I can't stand is the whole NME Indie scene. The women think that if they buy leggings from

Trying To Be Strong

Topshop and get their hair done at Toni & Guy they fit in with that scene. But the guys take on this whole role of, 'Oh yeah, I'm going to be Liam fucking Gallagher.'

I once made this guy cry who thought he was someone special, giving it the whole, 'Yeah, I'm into Oasis . . .' I was at The Hawley Arms pub in Camden, north London and this guy suddenly came out with, 'Your mum is a cunt.' He was a big guy in all the tight gear, giving it large.

I turned around to him and said, 'Just because I can't help the cunt I came out of, you can't help the cunt you came out of. You're a dick!'

The whole pub fell silent and everyone just turned around and looked at us. He just burst into tears and blurted out, 'You can't call my mum a cunt.' I shouted back, 'Now you know how it feels, you can't call my mum a cunt.'

I suddenly remembered where I was and put my hand to my mouth. I thought, 'You can't say the C word across a pub!' No one, least of all him, expected the girl who looks like a Cabbage Patch Kid to turn around and say something back, but why shouldn't I? Who do these people think they are? I'll tell you something, tight trousers don't make you tough!

People don't realise how much it hurts whensomeone has a go at my mum and dad. I think they think because we did *The Osbournes* it gives them the right to say all of that shit.

AFTER a while we had some good news – my mum seemed to be getting much better. She was finally winning her battle with the cancer.

One of her friends had given her this bracelet that had numbers all the way around. After each chemotherapy session, she would rip off a number. I remember going to visit her in hospital one day and seeing she had only one number left. She seemed so much brighter and that's when I knew that she was going to be OK.

We had all been so worried, but we were also so proud of the way she had fought it. My mum really is an inspiration.

But even though we'd had some happy news, unfortunately it was followed by some sad news that affected us all so badly.

We were devastated when our great family friend, Bobby, lost his own battle with cancer. I found out while I was supporting the singer Robbie Williams on his three-month tour of Europe. When I knew that Mum was getting better, I'd accepted the chance to perform before Robbie every night.

I have never seen anyone perform like him. He was amazing. These were big arenas in front of hundreds of thousands of people, and every night he got on that stage and captivated the audience. Grabbing and keeping the attention of so many people is not easy, especially when you're the only person on the stage. But he did it. Robbie's a cool guy. If we were staying in a venue for two nights, we'd always have a party under the stage after the first gig. It was so much fun.

But it was while we were in Denmark that I found out about dear, dear Bobby. Like my uncle Tony, Bobby was part of the family. He was Scottish and a roadie who had worked with my dad from his Black Sabbath days. Everyone in the music industry knew who he was and if there was a book about the world's best tour managers he would be in it – at number one, probably.

I was getting ready to go on stage when Big Dave, my 'manny', knocked on my dressing room door. When I opened it he said, 'Kelly, I need you to sit down.'

My first reaction was, 'Oh my God, my mum has taken a turn for the worse. Oh my God, she's died.'

Big Dave looked at me and said, 'Bobby has passed away.' I was just numb. I couldn't speak. Big Dave said, 'Kelly, did you understand? Bobby has died.' Then whoosh, it just hit me.

Bobby had died on the road, touring with my dad, just as he'd wanted. Mum and Dad were so upset. They loved him so much. In fact, I didn't know anyone who didn't think he was great.

Bobby had looked after me a lot when I was growing up – Uncle Tony and Bobby were like second dads to me. He worked until the end and that would have made him happy, I know. I went out on stage that night and performed for him.

His son works with our family today and he's training to do just what his dad did. I know Bobby would have been so proud.

PERFORMING with Robbie was a high point of my music career. It was an honour to tour with him and his fans were so lovely to me.

Being on the road was fun too. My mum's best friend, Lynn, was with me. One night a friend had come to see me in Edinburgh.

Fierce

We were staying on the top floor of this big glass-fronted hotel and my friend and I had got pissed in the hotel's 'honesty bar'. I'm sorry, but no one is going to be honest in an honesty bar. What everyone does is they go to the area where all the drinks are and pretend they're just having an orange juice. Then they hope no one sees them when they grab the vodka bottle and pour a shot in! By the end of the night, we were all calling it the 'dishonesty bar'. Far more appropriate.

We left the bar and started messing around with the video camera we'd got. We went up to Lynn's room on the top floor and banged on the door before running away. She threw open the door. Oh my God, I have never seen anyone so angry in all of my life. She was screaming hysterically, 'I thought someone was trying to break in through my window and I was going to get raped.'

'Lynn,' I said. 'We're on the fucking top floor. Who was going to rape you? Spiderman?'

My life was always full of highs and lows. And while it was brilliant touring with Robbie, I was about to come back to earth with a bump when my addiction to painkillers became a bigger problem than I could have envisaged.

CHAPTER TWELVE

NODDY

*At the beginning they gave me a sort of buzz.
Now they were making me fall asleep; it didn't
matter where I was.*

WHEN the cameras came back to film us for the second series it struck me that all the fun of being in *The Osbournes* had gone for me. It was a combination of things that made me start to hate being on the show. On a superficial level, the novelty of suddenly being able to walk into my favourite nightclubs after years of queuing down Sunset Boulevard wore off almost as soon as it had begun. So did the endless supply of freebies we were sent from various companies such as computer-game manufacturers because they wanted free publicity. It was crazy the amount of stuff we were given. I actually really struggled with the whole freebie thing because when I sat back and thought about it, I couldn't understand what we'd done to deserve a new games console or whatever else they were sending. As a family we were just living our lives, so why were we being sent free shit? It started to trouble me.

No one ever sent me clothes back then because everyone thought I was too fat. I was a UK size ten. A size ten. How is that too fat? Someone was actually sitting in a fancy design studio somewhere saying, 'Don't send Kelly Osbourne anything. She's a size ten and far too fat for our clothes.' I couldn't have given a shit about whether I got free clothes or not, I was more than happy to spend my own money on my own clothes. But I did start to become really self-conscious about my size.

Living in Los Angeles had always been a something I found difficult because I wasn't one of those girls with a fake tan and blonde hair (although I am naturally blonde, which is more than can be said for most LA girls). I don't have massive tits and super-long legs. From the moment we moved to LA when I was thirteen, I stood out because I wouldn't conform to what the majority of people living there perceive as beautiful: I'm short, I have milky white skin and I wear big knickers! People thought I was ugly because in America they're obsessed with physical perfection.

Don't get me wrong, I'm fully aware that the day I decided to do *The Osbournes* was the day I sold my soul to the devil, but recognising it didn't stop the pain. I found myself looking for something to numb my anxiety.

WHILE we filmed the second series of the show in the summer of 2002, my mum was in and out of hospital being treated for colon cancer and was undergoing chemotherapy the whole time. If I'd not slept with her at the hospital, I'd be at home. That's when my problems with Vicodin

'I'm fully aware that the day I decided to do **The Osbournes** *was the day I sold my soul to the devil, but recognising it didn't stop the pain. I found myself looking for something to numb my anxiety.'*

would be worse. I'd get up in the morning, open the white blinds and see a queue of photographers lining the street in the LA sunshine outside Doheny. I'd hear the camera crew wandering around the house and my heart would sink and I'd feel like total shit. I'd quit my job at the music management company, which meant I could go out every night if I wanted and, because the camera crew were simply recording our lives as they were, I could behave however I wanted. There were no rules.

By this point, I was taking Vicodin every time I went out – which was most nights – and then one morning, while we were filming the second series of the show in the summer, I woke up and took a Vicodin for breakfast. I don't know why I did it.

My bed – a silver four-poster – was in the middle of the room and I leaned out that morning and grabbed the small bottle of painkillers sitting on top of the table next to it. It wasn't that I wanted to get high. No – it was not ever, ever, ever about getting high. Vicodin made me feel like a different person because it blocked out the pain. And for the first time since I'd moved to America, I was starting to feel like I belonged and that I could cope with the show.

Eventually, swallowing one Vicodin when I woke up wasn't doing the trick any more so I quickly moved on to taking two and then three. Soon I was waking up, leaning out of my bed and emptying six into my hand and knocking them back. Then I'd have another six for lunch and another six for dinner. My friends started calling me Noddy because every time we went out, I would fall asleep due to the effects of the painkillers. While at the beginning they gave me a sort of buzz, they were now making me fall asleep; it didn't matter where I was.

I'd usually get home from a night out at 3 a.m. and go straight to bed and sleep until 4 p.m. When I woke up I'd grab a handful of pills, shove them in my mouth and swallow them before I'd even had chance to open my eyes properly. I didn't bother hiding my bottle of pills, instead I kept them on my bedside table. You want to hide something? Put it in the most obvious place and I guarantee no one will see it.

There would be the usual chaos going on outside my bedroom with the dogs barking, my mum chatting, my dad wandering around, and this was all being captured by the MTV camera crew. Truthfully, the film crew didn't want to work with me – they didn't like me. No one liked me, including my own family. My addiction to Vicodin was beginning to make me moody, difficult and hateful. Who wants to be around someone like that? I was constantly fighting with Jack – massive fights which usually ended in my smacking or punching him. No matter how angry he got though, he'd never hit me back, but he'd shout and I'd scream. It must have been horrendous for the film crew at times.

Behind my closed bedroom door, I'd pull myself out of my bed in the late afternoon, pad across the thick cream carpet to my en-suite bathroom where I'd run a bath and look for my phone to call my friends and find out where they were going out that night. Sometimes they would come over and we'd get ready at our house or I'd meet them somewhere on Sunset like The Roxy. By the time I left the house at 10 p.m., I'd usually taken about thirty tablets. Someone who'd never taken Vicodin before would almost certainly overdose after ten pills, let alone thirty.

I had built up a resistance over the months I'd started to take them and I was feeling no side-effects apart from constantly falling asleep. I was taking so many pills that during dinner or even in the noisiest clubs I would just doze off and my head would hit the table with a bang – I would literally nod off, hence my nickname Noddy. The music would be thumping around me and I'd be fast asleep in some corner somewhere.

On 14 September 2002, *The Osbournes* won an Emmy in the Outstanding Non-fiction Program (Reality) category, which was the first Emmy MTV had won in its twenty-one-year history. I went with my mum, who was very weak and still undergoing chemotherapy, to collect the award. I barely remember it. I was so high.

Some of my friends knew what I was taking and some didn't. By now, you might be wondering whether or not my mum and dad knew? They had their suspicions, but I denied it when they asked me and I was very good at lying about it. My mum would come into my bedroom and perch on the end of the bed and say, 'Kelly, my darling, are you taking something? What is it that you're doing? Please tell me. Please tell your mummy.'

I would just deny it. What could she do? I was seventeen and she had no proof.

Melinda and Big Dave had their suspicions too. But there was nothing they could do either because I just kept saying that everything was OK.

One night I sat in the middle of my bed with my back against the wall, looking at the Andy Warhol print of Marilyn Monroe I had hanging up, and thought, 'Kelly, you've got a problem.' That was probably the first time I'd addressed it in my own head. But by then it was too late and I was addicted. I was taking Vicodin because I had to: my body needed it and I was thinking I would die if I didn't take it. Those pills were consuming my whole life.

THERE was another problem too. The music career I'd launched in 2002 was starting to make me miserable. By now I was at the height of my addiction, taking up to fifty painkillers a day. At fifty a day I could have overdosed of course, but I didn't want to. There were times it would have helped me escape the misery of my addiction, which was now making me more unhappy than before I'd started to take pills.

In the autumn of 2003, we were filming the third series of *The Osbournes* and I'd signed to the record label Sanctuary. The only real positive at that time was being asked to do a duet with my father on a cover of the Black Sabbath hit 'Changes'. It was a song I'd always loved and being able to do it with my father was just an honour. I am his biggest fan. It was released at the beginning of December and Dad and I were going to the UK to promote it.

A couple of nights before we were due to fly out I'd gone out with my friends to a club. I was permanently out of it from Vicodin at this point and I'd come home and passed out across my bed, fully clothed with my bedroom light still on.

As I lay in bed, completely out of it, my mum, worried, had tip-toed into my bedroom. I don't know why she'd bothered to

'As I lay there my mum kept repeating,

"Kelly, what are you doing to yourself?

What have you taken? Tell me!"

It shocked the hell out of me and it

shocked the hell out of my mother.'

Fierce

be quiet because I was too gone to notice. I woke up to my mum, in her silk pyjamas, sitting on my bottom with her legs at either side of my waist pounding my back and screaming, 'Kelly. Wake up, Kelly.' I was literally soaking wet from my own piss. I was covered in it and my mum was beating my back because she thought I'd stopped breathing. As I lay there my mum kept repeating, 'Kelly, what are you doing to yourself? What have you taken? Tell me!' It shocked the hell out of me and it shocked the hell out of my mother. Of course she had her fears, but there was nothing she could do because the next morning, when she asked me again what I'd taken, I denied it and told her I was just drunk. Two days later, Dad and I flew out to the UK and we stayed at Welders while we promoted the single.

On the 8 December 2003, I was booked on the Channel Four chat show *Richard & Judy* to talk about the single. I'd left Dad at home with the MTV crew who'd come over with us and Uncle Tony. I used to watch Richard and Judy when they hosted *This Morning* on ITV when I was off sick from school. So not only was I so excited to be back in the UK, I was even more excited that I was going to be a guest on their show.

The show was filmed in Kennington, south London, and Big Dave had come with me. It was live from 5 p.m. to 6 p.m., so I was sitting in my dressing room at about 4 p.m. when I got a call from Mum. She asked me if I was sitting down, which instantly made my heart start thumping. She said, 'Kelly, your father has had an accident and we need to get you to the hospital.' I just burst into tears. Me and Big Dave ran out of the studio and jumped into the car that had been waiting to take us back to

Welders after the show. While we were in the car, Uncle Tony called and said Dad had been riding one of his quad bikes in the grounds, crashed and fallen off. My dad had a collection of quad bikes and we always used to ride them in the garden and we often used to crash. But this time it was serious and he'd been rushed into hospital.

The driver took us to Paddington Station where we sat on a train for forty minutes before getting back into a car again to Wexham Park Hospital, just outside Slough. The whole time I was worried about what state Dad would be in when we got there. I ran into the hospital nearly an hour and a half after my mum had first called and found my dad in the intensive care unit alongside about twelve or thirteen other patients all wired up to God knows how many machines.

As I stood there, staring at him helplessly, I could feel my legs shaking and I was shivering. It was awful. Really fucking awful. I thought, 'Is my dad going to die?' A doctor came over and introduced himself before guiding me by the arm into a private room where he asked my permission to operate as I was the next of kin. He told me that Dad had cracked vertebrae in his neck, broken eight ribs, shattered his collarbone and was suffering from blood on his lungs.

'Our main concern . . .' the doctor started as he eased me gently into a chair. When he saw the shock on my face he started again: 'We are concerned about the blood supply to his left arm as a result of a punctured main artery. We have seventy-two hours to get the blood back or we'll have to amputate.'

The whole time I was repeating back to him, 'Please just do

Fierce

whatever you have to do to save my dad. Please save my dad.' The doctor then lowered his voice and added, 'Be prepared that this may be the last time that you might be able to speak to your daddy because your daddy might not make it.'

I walked in and my dad was talking to the nurses. He was on so much medication he seemed OK and he kept pressing the morphine button so it would go into his system quicker – bloody typical of him. He was pointing at me and then the nurses saying, 'Don't let them fuck up my tattoos, Kel.'

I don't know what he thought they were going to do. But as I stood there holding his hand by the bedside, all of a sudden he started to make these gargling noises and then these brown bubbles started to come out of his mouth. There was a deafening flat-line noise coming from the machine he was attached to. The medical team raced to him and started working on him and I was practically carried out backwards by two doctors, kicking my legs and screaming because I didn't want to leave him.

After they'd managed to stabilise him, I called Mum and told her that Dad had gone into surgery to repair his arm, but by then Uncle Tony had told her the extent of Dad's injuries and she was preparing to fly to London on her own. While she was taking the eleven-hour flight to the UK, the doctors battled to save Dad's arm by taking a vein from his right arm and putting it in his left to replace the damaged artery.

I spent the night at the hospital with Uncle Tony pacing up and down and hoping my dad would be OK. Photographers started to arrive outside and soon there was a whole bunch of them huddled together on the freezing December evening.

When my mum arrived the next day she was bundled through the pack and into the hospital. Dad was on a respirator, unable to breathe on his own, and there was every tube imaginable coming out from all over his body. By this point, the newspapers had got wind of the story and the *Daily Mirror* front page said: 'Ozzy in quad bike horror.'

Uncle Tony explained to me that the bike had landed on Dad after he'd fallen off, when he had ridden into a pot-hole hidden by leaves. The security man who was with him at the time had actually had to revive my father twice. We were all so worried.

My mum was now in remission from cancer, and in the autumn of 2003 had started filming her chat show, *The Sharon Osbourne Show*, in the States. She had to abandon filming so she could be with my dad. After two days – we were waiting for the dreaded seventy-two hours to pass, when we'd find out whether my father had lost his arm or not – I flew back to America to cover for her. I didn't want to leave Dad, but I agreed to go only for a couple of days before flying back to the UK to be with him again.

During that time, Mum kept me up to date on his condition and we were so pleased when the doctors told us the vein had taken and the arm wouldn't need to be amputated. But that wasn't the end; Dad was unable to breathe on his own and was still on a respirator. As I flew back to Los Angeles, Jack and Aimee, unable to bear being so far away, were travelling to the UK to be with him. Recording Mum's show wasn't a problem – it was in a studio on Sunset and not far from Doheny. But I

Fierce

desperately wanted to get back. Throughout this whole period I was still popping my Vicodin pills. I had a permanent stash on me.

When I returned to the hospital, Mum, Jack and Aimee had pretty much been covering the visits in shifts. Welders was a twenty-minute drive away and Uncle Tony had been ferrying them backwards and forwards. My father's sisters came to visit with my half-brother and -sister, Louis and Jessica, who flew in from Ireland. Colin Newman came and so did Dad's writing partner, Mark Hudson.

Mum would catnap beside him and me, Jack, Aimee, Uncle Tony and Big Dave all took it in turns to sit and talk to him. On the eighth day after the operation, they finally took him off the ventilator. His breathing wasn't great, but he was conscious. During those eight days our single had gone to number one in the UK charts and I'd been absolutely desperate for him to wake up so I could tell him. His breathing started to get better but he still couldn't speak properly. On the tenth day after the accident, I stood by his bed and said, 'Dad, our single is number one.' He responded by holding up one of his fingers as a sign that he'd understood. The tears poured down my cheeks. He was obviously so pleased for us and wanted to let me know, but it was the only thing he could do.

I said, 'I love you, Dadda.'

Dad's accident and the daily trips to the hospital had left us all so exhausted that Mum planned a little overnight trip to London to give us a break before we spent Christmas in the hospital with Dad. My mum liked to make Christmas special for us all and it was a really nice break while the nurses took care of my dad in hospital. But when we got back the next morning we had a shock. Dad was sitting on the edge of the bed with a collar around his neck and tears in his eyes saying, 'Sharon, I want to come out.'

The nurses had said March, and we all wanted him to stay in the hospital because he wasn't ready to leave. Me, Jack and Aimee were all in tears as we huddled around Dad trying to persuade him to stay and get the care he needed. I was pleading, 'Dad, you have to stay in. Please.' But he asked the hospital staff for the papers that he needed to sign himself out, and there was nothing any one of us could do. We'd have to cope.

Me and Mum slept with him in the spare room throughout Christmas, Mum lying in the cramped single bed next to Dad and me on the floor in case he rolled out. It was crazy, but it was what my dad wanted. Of course he was being difficult and insisting on doing more than he should have been, like hobbling around with a stick and not resting, so in the end Mum packed the rest of us back to LA. She stayed to look after him.

I flew back on my own and during the flight – despite being out of it on Vicodin – I decided I didn't want to take the tablets any more. I'd been worried sick about my father after the accident, I hated the horrible feeling of coming down from the pills during every flight and I wanted to be in control of my life.

When I got back to LA I vowed that that was it. But I still had a big stash at the house, so instead of throwing them away, I decided not to buy any more when they ran out. It wasn't until the end of February that that happened, which gives you an idea of how

‘

On the tenth day after the accident,

I stood by his bed and said,

"Dad, our single is number one."

He responded by holding up one of his

fingers as a sign that he'd understood.

’

The tears poured down my cheeks.

many pills I had. True to my word, I prepared to come off them on my own. This was a stupid idea.

Vicodin is an opiate and is stored in your muscles, so as soon as I tried to stop taking them it made my body ache as the drugs gradually began to leave my system. I felt very sick and the longer I went without taking another pill the harder it got.

I was scrunched up in a ball on my bed in Doheny, shivering like crazy, with goose bumps all over my body. I couldn't bear it. That feeling would have lasted two weeks. But after two days I gave up.

Because I'd wanted to stop taking them, my usual stash had run dry so, in a panic, I called the guy who had given me my first tablet more than two and a half years earlier. He agreed to meet me straight away, and I got in my car and drove the five minutes to Sunset where we'd arranged to meet outside a store.

Mum and Dad had now flown back to LA so she could finish filming *The Sharon Osbourne Show*. My dad was improving and Mum was in talks to be a judge on a new ITV show called *The X Factor*. We were also preparing to start the merry-go-round of press for the third series of *The Osbournes*.

On the Friday after I had bought my pills on Sunset I was sitting in my bedroom when my mum stormed in and chucked a whole bunch of photographs at me. They scattered on the bed and I looked down and saw images of me handing over money to my dealer and taking something from him. I'd been caught buying drugs. My mum was pacing the room shouting, 'You're a fucking liar, Kelly. You've been fucking lying to us and we're sick of your bullshit.'

I sat there with my mouth closed not saying a word. What could I say? My heart was pounding, but at the same time I felt a sense of relief. I knew I needed help.

My mum was on a mission. She made me tell her who'd been giving the pills to me and got him on the phone. She bollocked him like I've never heard her bollock anyone before. I didn't even fight back. I just listened and looked at her. I thought, 'Kelly Osbourne, you've been busted.'

It turned out that earlier that day, the *News of the World* had sent the pictures of me scoring drugs to our family publicist and they had contacted my mum. Now she had the proof – one hundred per cent proof – and there was nothing I could do but go into rehab.

I am in no position to tell someone whether to take drugs or not take drugs, but I can tell you the reality.

The reality is this: every day is a struggle when you're an addict. In the back of your mind you're always thinking, OK if something shitty happens, am I going to turn to the drugs again? That is a huge burden for anyone. I suffer terrible anxiety since I've given up drugs. I can sit in a room and feel like the walls are closing in on me. That feeling will probably stay with me for ever.

I owe the photographer who exposed me in the newspaper a massive thank you! He changed my life. The day I was actually forced to think about what I was doing to myself, my family and my friends (and those photographs made me do that), changed me for ever. Because even when you go back to drugs, the first time you're made to face the fact that what you're doing is seriously damaging you, that feeling never, never, never goes away.

Noddy

CHAPTER THIRTEEN

NO VACATION

Drugs made me so selfish. They were all-consuming.

O N the day I was checking into rehab, my parents decided
to go on *Larry King Live*. It's a hugely popular talk show
on the TV channel CNN. They had decided that they wanted
to pre-empt the *News of the World* story and announce to the
world that I was checking into rehab. I hated them for doing
that. I really did. I think they did it because they felt massively
guilty that another one of their children was going into rehab.
They also wanted people to know the true story. I was really
angry with them. I wanted just a bit of time to clear my head
before the *News of the World* printed the story. But Mum and
Dad going on that show stopped that. While they headed off to
the studio, Jack, Melinda and Big Dave stayed with me at home
– probably to make sure I wouldn't try and run away.

We were still filming the third series of *The Osbournes* so
all the MTV crew were still with us and they were hanging
around the house. They had been with us long enough to know
when it was wise to turn off the cameras. They had always

been respectful in that way. The show was still at the height of its popularity, so we were being followed everywhere by photographers outside the house as well as those inside for the show.

Mum and Dad caused a bit of a distraction when they pulled out of Doheny to go to the studio, so quite a few of the photographers followed them. My parents had come into my bedroom before they left. They both looked so worried as they kissed and hugged me goodbye. Dad was hovering behind Mum with a look of terror on his face. I didn't really know what was going on. The whole thing had been a whirlwind and if it hadn't been for the photographer who had shopped me, I would have been busy getting ready to go out with my friends to pop a load more pills that night.

Mum had spent the morning putting calls into rehab facilities – she had done it so many times before for my dad and once for Jack. I felt fucking sorry for my mum. It was agreed that I would go to the Promises facility on the coast in Malibu, which is a twenty-one-mile strip of coastline west of Los Angeles. A lot of Hollywood actors live there with their homes overlooking the beaches.

To stop the photographers following us, the MTV guys said they would take me in the back of their van. The paps who were permanently camped outside our house were used to seeing them coming and going, so they wouldn't suspect anything different. I needed that. I couldn't have coped with a load of photographers and their camera bulbs flashing in my face as I walked into the rehab clinic. I felt bloody humiliated.

'Mum had spent the morning putting calls into rehab facilities – *she had done it so many times before for my dad and once for Jack.*'

Jack came and sat in the back of the van with me. He was the best person to accompany me to the facility. It had been nearly a year since he had checked into Las Encinas Hospital, Pasadena, California to get treatment for his drink and drug addiction. He had stayed clean ever since. Around the same time, my dad had made a pact with Jack that if he got clean, Dad would try too. He had also kept his promise.

Do you know how my father apologised to my mother for all of the drugs he'd taken? I think it's an important part of recovery to say sorry to everyone who has been affected by your actions. My mum was taking a shit one afternoon at Doheny and my father walked into the bathroom and said, 'Sharon?'

'Yeah, Ozzy,' Mum said.

'I love you and I'm sorry.'

My mum was wiping her fucking arse. I'm not fucking lying.

Dad now wears his circular sunglasses out of habit – they're his trademark – but originally he used to wear them so people couldn't see his pupils and know that he was high. Not any more.

As Jack and Dad were celebrating their one-year anniversary of being clean, I was checking into rehab for the first time on 2 April 2004. At the time, I was so wrapped up in myself that I wasn't even thinking about how Jack and dad had stayed clean. I was lost in myself. I didn't believe they would stay sober, if I'm honest. But my God, I'm so fucking proud of them.

As I was about to discover, it's the hardest thing you can do. For both of them to stay sober is just amazing. Especially Jack. He was just seventeen when he got clean and he stuck to it through his most impressionable years, when it would have been so easy to relapse because all his friends were drinking and smoking. But he didn't, and that says a hell of a lot about his strength of character.

As we pulled out of the drive, I was crying my eyes out. I just didn't know what I was going into. There had been many times when I'd gone with Mum to take Dad to rehab, but it ended at the door. This time I was going to be walking through those doors and I really didn't know what I was going to face. I was terrified.

Jack sat in the van next to me and wrapped a blanket around my shoulders. I sobbed during the entire forty-minute journey. I had felt so unbelievably miserable being addicted to Vicodin that there was part of me that was relieved and thanking God it was over. I kept repeating to myself: 'I'm going to get help. I'm going to get help.'

But stupidly there was another part of me that thought, 'OK, I'll do the thirty days, get out and go back on them and hang out with my friends.' None of it made any sense.

As Jack checked me into Promises, Mum and Dad were about to appear on *Larry King Live*.

I saw them on the TV in the rehab facility as I was being checked in. It broke my heart. I saw it as them trying to get themselves out of trouble. I knew I was in the public eye and there are very few secrets when you are, but I still didn't understand why they had to go on TV. They didn't want people to write bullshit, I get that now. But I didn't then.

After Mum had been tipped off by the newspaper, they'd both gone through my bedroom. They had found five hundred pills

'There had been many times when I'd gone with mum to take dad to rehab, but it ended at the door. This time I was going to be walking through those doors and I really didn't know what I was going to face. I was terrified.'

Fierce

scattered around the room – under my bed, in my handbag, in bottles by my bed.

'The amount of pills I found in Kelly's bag was astounding,' Dad told Larry.

'Literally, a couple of hours ago she was admitted into rehab,' Mum added.

MY first impression of Promises was that it looked like a bit of a joke. It was a fuck-off mansion on the cliff on the Malibu coast. For a lot of people checking in there, it's a lot nicer than their own homes.

It might work for some people, but for me it was like a villa you stay in on your holidays, but there isn't any alcohol to drink by the pool. The facility prides itself on being designed for clients who are accustomed to luxury but as I was going to find out, I needed to be taken out of my comfort zone to be able to fight my addiction to drugs.

There were wooden balconies overlooking the ocean with green cushioned recliner chairs. The sun was shining and I felt like I was on the first day of my holiday. That soon changed, I can tell you.

I'd had times when I was starting to come down from Vicodin, but I'd always been able to take some more pills to stop the withdrawal.

This time I was going to have to detox my body off the drug before I could start my treatment. I was put in a room on my

No Vacation

own – a scenario I would have to go through a few times in the future too. It was like a hotel room with a big bed and white linen. It was what it said on the tin. It was luxurious.

Because I had been heavily addicted, the doctors gave me some drugs to help take the edge off my withdrawal. It was still the worst thing that I've ever been through.

I LAY in bed with the sun streaming through the wooden blinds at the window and my whole body just seemed to go through some sort of shock. I was shaking uncontrollably, my joints ached. They really fucking ached. I was sweating and I felt sick. I couldn't sleep at all. I felt fucking awful. Really fucking awful. If someone had said to me, you can take some Vicodin now, I would have jumped at the chance. I would have done anything to stop that withdrawal. I was crying with the pain and there was nowhere I could go to stop it. There was nothing I could do to stop it apart from roll around in bed and suffer the agony. It was like the worst flu you've ever suffered.

It took me nearly a week to detox from the drugs and every bit of it was hell. Once I'd got through that, it really did feel like I was on holiday. I had acupuncture, I was given a personal trainer and I had a massage every day.

But even though I'd gone through the pain and horror of coming off the drugs I just didn't feel I had tackled the underlying problem of my addiction. I left there after thirty days thinking, 'This is bullshit.'

But I started to get my life back together. I wanted to concentrate on my music career and I felt really clear-headed.

Fierce

Despite my earlier reluctance when I'd checked out of Promises, I felt like I was doing really well. 'One Word' was going to be released in the April. I recorded a really cool video for that song. I loved it. It was shot in black and white and was based on scenes from the French cult sci-fi movie *Alphaville, une étrange aventure de Lemmy Caution*, which was about a secret agent. It was so much fun.

But after the single came out, I suffered a severe setback. Something I'd said in private had got leaked to the press. Looking back it was so bloody stupid, but at the time I felt I couldn't trust anyone any more. I can't even remember what it was that was said. I started taking drugs again. Pills were just a phone call away. All I had to do was dial the number.

I was staying at Welders in May 2005 while I was promoting my new album, but I wasn't really in a fit state to be doing it. Mum and Dad had work commitments in the UK too and one Sunday we were at home together. I had taken a load of Vicodin when I'd woken up that morning and I was pretty out of it. The three of us were having a Sunday roast and I just nodded off at the table. I woke up to my parents looking over me in floods of tears. They were thinking, 'Here we go again.'

Mum said, 'Oh, Kel, what are you doing?'

Dad had his arm around her and was saying: 'Kel, listen to me, man, you've got to get help. You've just fucking nodded off on us.'

I had a flight booked to go back to LA before returning to the UK to continue promoting the album. On the plane I started to detox. The problem was that the Vicodin usually lasted between six to twelve hours, so whenever I used to fly from America to

No Vacation

the UK – which is an eleven-hour flight – I'd often fall asleep and wake up on a come-down that meant I'd shiver and feel sick and my whole body would ache.

I wrapped the flimsy airplane blanket around me and rested my head on my own pillow – that I took on every flight – but I felt terrible. I was just curled up, waiting for the plane to land. But for some reason, I didn't take more pills to relieve my come-down.

As I stood shivering at LAX Airport waiting to go through passport control, I knew I couldn't do it any more. I owed it to myself and my family to try and get help.

When I walked out of the airport I got the driver to drive me to Las Encinas Hospital – the same facility that Jack had gone into.

After checking me in, the facility called my parents and told them I'd gone into rehab for thirty days. Just over a year after my first visit, I was in rehab again for the second time on 2 June 2005.

Las Encinas was completely different to Promises. It certainly wasn't as luxurious. When I walked in it smelt like a hospital. The rooms were really basic. Some of the rooms were similar to something a grandma would have in her home – red curtains and flowery sheets on the bed.

They put me on a medical detox for three days, which meant all my belongings were taken off me. I was left in bed to go through the horrendous side-effects of cold turkey again. This time I had such bad night sweats. Every part of me was sweating, but at the same time I was shivering – really, really shivering.

The one thing that Las Encinas taught me was to be humble. Drugs had made me so selfish. They were all-consuming. All I thought about from the moment I woke up was when would I need to take my next Vicodin? Would I have enough Vicodin? When would I need to see my dealer to buy more Vicodin? When you look at it like that, it's fucking ridiculous to fill your head with just that. But when you're an addict, you do. After a week I moved into a room with another girl and I got my belongings back. It wasn't the cleanest room and my mattress was dirty. The girl I was sharing with was self-harming and cutting herself.

During this time I was really pissed off with my family because they hadn't come to visit me. But deep down I knew why. They were really, really mad with me. They were absolutely done with me. In the run-up to checking into rehab I had been unbearable in every possible way. I was arguing with everyone and I hated everything. Sometimes someone would just say 'morning' to me and I'd find an excuse to snap at them. I was a selfish person. I couldn't blame them for not coming to see me.

After thirty days of being in the facility, I actually felt really positive when I left. I was confident that I could stay clean but I lasted a matter of weeks. I just couldn't do it. One afternoon I called the same dealer I had met all those years earlier and he brought over a bottle of Vicodin. It was as simple as that.

The first time I popped one of those pills I felt so much better again. The anxiety I was feeling just disappeared. It was the easy option.

I should have been promoting my album. I should have been excited about performing but instead I was back on the pills and I was back to being fucking miserable again. I'd convinced myself that I'd needed pills to get through my life.

This time my parents didn't mess around. They knew the pattern and when they realised what was happening, they checked me into the UCLA Medical Institution in Los Angeles. I was checked on to the psychiatric ward. It is known for having a good alcohol and drug treatment programme. Years later, the singer Britney Spears would also be admitted onto the same ward.

Mum and Dad drove me there and they were both sobbing in the car. They were going through the motions to some extent, though. They didn't know whether I was going to stick to it or not. I was sitting in the back seat and I was actually shaking with nerves. I was absolutely terrified. We pulled into the car park and my parents checked me in. I was effectively going into a mental institution.

The ward was divided up into individual rooms. It smelt sterile and it was really rundown. It needed a fresh coat of paint. On that first night I was put into a room on my own. I was so frightened; it was full of crazy people. All night patients were screaming – really screaming. As I curled up on my bed in a tight ball, I started to suffer the effects of withdrawing from the drugs. The whole time the air was filled with ear-piercing screams. They went right through me. I thought those patients would come into my room.

I didn't leave my room for five days. For three days I simply couldn't move, but after that I was still too terrified to go out.

Fierce

'The first time I popped one of those pills I felt so much better again.

The anxiety I was feeling just disappeared.

It was the easy option.'

No Vacation

The only people I would see would be the nurses who brought my food in and gave me my medication. I had no other human contact.

Put it this way, I had a lot of time to think. It was just me and my thoughts. I didn't do the group therapy or anything. Instead, I decided to write down how I felt. I wrote pages of stuff and I found it really therapeutic. Afterwards, I would ask the nurses to burn my words. I didn't want anyone, NOT ANYONE, to read them.

In the second week I did the therapy and the sessions. They were so intense. I stayed on the mental ward for two weeks. I can safely say it's one of the scariest things I have ever done. But it's also one of the best things I've done too. I was twenty years old and I was in a mental institution. It changed my life for ever.

When I checked out of the hospital, I made a really big decision. I decided that I didn't want to live in LA any more, I wanted to move to London.

Jack and I were watching the music channel VH1 at Doheny one day and a show called *Where Are They Now?* came on. That show had a crazy effect on me. It basically goes back and tracks down stars who were once massive, but find themselves working on a hot-dog stall when the fame bubble has burst.

I turned to Jack and said, 'In a couple of years they're going to be doing that show on me and you.'

The thought of being on that show made me feel like all my worst nightmares were going to come true. I didn't want to be one of those LA kids – the celebrity daughter of whoever, living in their parents' guest house, driving in the latest car they'd been given and filling their days shopping. I didn't want to look back on my life and feel like I had cheated myself out of being successful because I had been too successful when I was a kid.

It wasn't an easy decision, and I think Mum felt like I was abandoning her, but I moved to London because I had to get away from my family. Not in a bad way, because they weren't doing anything horrible to me. I just needed to not be an Osbourne for a while. Mum is my manager and my mum and I needed time to figure out who I was without having a million people telling me the answer.

I also needed a break from all the family dramas. Our home was one of those houses where people would always be coming and going. There would be the usual dramas: Dad wasn't talking to Mum or Jack had fallen out with Mum or whatever – I didn't want to be a part of that bullshit any more. I called it getting away from the 'LA dramatics'. For some reason I was always taking on my mum's battles for her. Not that she ever asked me to. But she would come out with crazy stuff in interviews and I would leap in to support her. Plus LA wasn't my place. In London I'd always felt comfortable and accepted. I just needed to fuck off for a while, so I did.

I packed my stuff and got on a plane. It was only as I took off from LAX that it struck me that I only knew a handful of people in London. But it felt like an adventure and I couldn't wait for it to start.

No Vacation

CHAPTER FOURTEEN

CLUB KITCHEN

*I missed my family terribly when I was in London,
but as I'd created my own little life, the horrible
homesickness pain didn't feel so bad.*

WHEN I first moved to London I rented a flat in St John's
Wood, North London. I liked the area. It's residential
and very leafy and pretty.

After a few weeks, the house Mum and Dad owned and rented
out in West London became available so they said I could move
in. It's a three-storey house with a cute garden in a gated area, so
it instantly felt really secure. It's not a massive house, but it was
my home and I loved it. The neighbours were great and made
me feel really welcome. I'd never known anything like it. They
were the sort of people who would knock on the door and ask if
I needed anything.

A few months later when I turned twenty-one, Mum and Dad
gave me the house as a birthday present. I consider myself really
fucking lucky for that. A lot of people look at me and think, 'Her
parents just give her everything.' But apart from the house, they

haven't given me money for anything since we started doing *The Osbournes*. They opened the door for us, sure. But we had to walk through it.

In those first few weeks I felt really scared about being in a new city. I'd never actually lived in London. My time in the UK had always been spent at Welders, which is about a forty-minute drive from central London.

Luckily my best friend from school, Sammy, was living nearby because she was training to be a nurse and Fleur was always about because her parents lived near London. Being able to hang out with them again was one of the best things about moving to England.

I was also discovering new likes and dislikes all the time. Like not having to worry about putting make-up on before leaving the house. That was a big like! The best part was moving away from a city where everyone judges you on your appearance to being able to express myself just how I wanted. You're allowed to be quirky when you're in London. It doesn't matter if you're not stick-thin or if you're not carrying the latest designer handbag. I loved that. It didn't matter that I didn't fit into a certain box and, for the first time in a long time, I didn't feel insecure.

The biggest thing I learned was that I could do things without my family. Before I lived in London I didn't think I could live without them. I also learned it was OK to make mistakes. I didn't always know how the fucking central heating worked or how to sort out my bills but I learned – that was half the fun.

Fierce

IDECIDED the only way I was going to make friends was to go out – every night. I'd call Sammy and Fleur and get them to come to different pubs and clubs with me. I didn't know where the cool places were to hang out, I used to just find out where the indie nights were at different bars and go along.

On one of those nights out I met this really cool girl called Margo. I invited her over to my house one Sunday afternoon to hang out. She came over and brought a guy called Sharif with her.

I'd got bored waiting for them and so, to keep myself entertained, I'd put on my favourite yellow raincoat and put the hood up. I was lying on the floor listening to music when the doorbell went and I called to them to walk in.

Sharif said seeing me lying on my back in the middle of my lounge singing some cheesy pop song was one of the funniest things he'd ever seen. We became the best of friends straight away. I call him the boy that never went home because, since that day, we've lived together. He moved into my spare room that week. Sharif became my first-ever flatmate. That in itself was something I had never experienced.

Sharif is a year older than me and works as a design consultant for big stores wanting to rebrand. He is the funniest and most fun person I've ever hung out with. There is not one person in this fucking world who understands me more than Sharif. We do everything together. He became my house husband.

Club Kitchen

When I'm sad he cheers me up. He has got this amazing way of, when I'm freaking out about something – which happens a lot – making me look at all the angles so that I don't panic.

Life is never boring when he is around. We can be sitting in the house on an evening watching TV and Sharif will suddenly say, 'Let's fucking dress up!' He'll be running around the house pulling clothes from all the cupboards. One night he dressed up as Naomi Campbell and then there was Posh Spice – he does the best fucking impressions. Whenever he goes out, I'll sit for ages cutting out pictures from magazines of people who we think are really funny like the *Big Brother* winners. Or I'll cut out pictures of girls who purposely don't wear knickers when they're out so they get their fanny papped.

Then, when Sharif gets home and goes for a piss, he'll lift up the toilet seat and I'll have stuck a whole bunch of pictures on the inside of the lid. There was also the time I found a life-size poster of Naomi Campbell and laid it in bed next to him. When he woke up he jumped out of his skin!

Sharif and I were in Vegas and two of our friends suddenly decided to get married. We went to this celebratory dinner first and I looked around and saw that Sharif was crying at the table. I said, 'Sharif, why are you crying?'

He was being all dramatic saying, 'Because I know I'm going to die alone.'

I said, 'No, no you won't, I'll be there.'

Sharif said, 'I know . . . that's why I'm crying!'

It was the funniest thing I'd ever heard! I thought I would piss myself laughing.

Fierce

Sharif and I went out all the time when he first moved into my house. We'd hang out in Camden and go to The Hawley Arms. Amy Winehouse would be in there and it was always fun seeing her. I'd already met Amy a couple of years earlier at the Brit Awards. I had really massive tits at the time. Like, they were a cup size E or something. When I gain weight it goes everywhere, but particularly on my tits. It was the beginning of the night and I was wearing a red Marc Jacobs dress. Amy just came up to me and said, 'All right, Kel. You've got great tits.'

I'd never met her before. I didn't really know who she was because I was still living in LA at the time. But I instantly loved her and we became friends.

I was supposed to be presenting an award that night and I was meant to be sitting at another table but my mum was worried about me or something and swapped me with Aimee. So I got bumped off to another table miles away from the stage, so I got really pissed to piss her off.

Meeting Amy was fun. It sounds like I'm protecting her, but I'm not. The Amy that I know – the Amy that I'm so privileged and lucky to know – is not the Amy in the media and who people talk about. I truly believe that the only reason she does drugs is because it's the only thing she has control of in her life.

I love her music – but that's not why I love Amy. She gives the best advice. All talented people have troubles because they can't come to terms with it. I've often thought that about my dad. He's so fucking talented – maybe that's why he's had a problem with drugs.

The great thing about moving to my new house was that I instantly felt part of a little community. People don't think that London has a community feel, but I disagree. It really does. Kate Moss didn't live far away and Davinia Taylor and Sadie Frost were just around the corner. I'd met Kate for the first time at Elton John's White Tie and Tiara Ball when I was seventeen. I was on Elton's table with Mum, Dad, David Furnish and the artist Sam Taylor-Wood.

I was sitting next to Kate and I instantly thought she was great. I call Kate a 'tornado of fun'. She comes into a room and she brightens it up and that's just the way she is. People can say, 'Oh she is too old to do what she does and be a mum.' But Kate is a fantastic mum. She has really good morals when it comes to her friends. She doesn't tolerate meanness. If she feels someone is not being treated properly or is being bullied, she will always, always stick up for them.

Going out can be a bit of a nightmare when you're with a whole bunch of people who are in the public eye. You don't want people staring or taking pictures. It makes everyone feel really uncomfortable. All I ever want to do is have a couple of drinks and a laugh. When we're all in London – me, Sharif, Kate, Davinia, the hairdresser James Brown, 'Jimmy B' and Fran Cutler – we call a meeting of 'Club Kitchen'. That's when we go to one of our houses, play music and have a few drinks – all in the kitchen. We always have a wicked night and no one gets hassled. I love those nights because I can make a real fool of myself and not worry about being judged.

I learned pretty quickly some valuable lessons about who

Fierce

my real friends were when I moved to London. I was quite shocked by how people treated me just because they thought I had money. I do consider myself very lucky. I am not broke and of course I am over-privileged. In that respect, I have a great life. But some people have really taken advantage of that and it has been a problem for me. People seem to think they can take what's mine because they feel I haven't had to work for it.

So-called friends have actually come into my home and stolen things, just because they thought they could. Just little things like pictures or whatever! Why the fuck would you do that? They've also asked me to lend them money. They'd say, 'Can you lend me five hundred pounds to pay the rent?' I have lent shit-loads to so-called friends. So much, I have no idea. In the beginning I lent the money because I couldn't bear the thought of people going around saying, 'Kelly Osbourne is a tight bitch.' Maybe I felt embarrassed about having money. Fuck knows.

But not everyone paid it back. And then I didn't hear from them again. For a while I carried on and thought, 'OK, just take the money and I will leave you to be the moral person. If not, I won't speak to you again.' But then I stopped doing it. Of course, I know who my close friends are now and I would always help them. But in those early days I had to learn very quickly. Yeah, it pissed me off. Yeah, it upset me at times. But fuck, yeah, it made me realise you can't be seen to help everyone. It's just not going to happen, I can tell you.

People tend to gravitate towards me when they need help and are in the shit. I don't know why. I actually think people have the same image of me as they do my mum. People always see

'Of course, *I know who my close friends are now* and *I would always help them.* **But in those early days** **I learned very quickly.**'

her as being the person in control who can sort out everyone's problems. They're right about Mum. But I think the image they have of me is completely wrong. Maybe it's because I have an old head on young shoulders and speak my mind.

IT was my twenty-first birthday a couple of months after I'd moved to London. I was enjoying my new little life and I really wasn't bothered about doing anything to celebrate. But Mum and Claire, who works in Mum's office in the UK, said I should do something. Claire is the person I go to for advice in the UK. She's like an older sister. In America I used to chat to Melinda. I always go to Claire and Melinda when I know I can't go to Mum. Sometimes Mum's just too close to the situation. She's all, 'Oh, my poor baby. Oh, I'm hurting . . .'

Whereas Claire will always give me impartial advice. She will say, 'OK, you did fuck up. But this is what we can do to sort it out.'

Sometimes, when she's mad with other people, I take the piss and say, 'Don't go all Essex, Claire.' She's very straight-talking and doesn't mess about. Claire works with Lynn in mum's office in North London and looks after our family's UK affairs. They are amazing. I'm so grateful for everything they do.

I have never known Lynn not to be working with my family. She met Mum just after she'd had Aimee. Lynn taught me how to type when I was about five – well, she said I was typing. I would go into the office and she would sit me on her knee and let me bash the keyboard. Then she would print out the pieces of paper and try and find random words I'd typed.

Mum and Dad have people in their lives – friends and colleagues – that have been with them since they first met. I think it says a lot about them that people still want to work with them after so many years. My parents have always taught me about how it's important to treat those closest to you with respect. It's thanks to them that I have Lynn and Claire in London and they really do look after me.

Claire suggested I should have my twenty-first birthday at the restaurant Sketch, which is just off Regent Street in central London. It's quite fancy, but she hired a private room and filled it with all my favourite things, like my closest friends and favourite food. She organised it all and it was the best birthday party I've ever had – still is. It was small – she only invited thirty people. But there were my thirty closest friends and family in the entire world and it was such fun. Mum, Dad and Jack were there. Claire and Lynn came with Sammy and Fleur and a whole bunch of other friends. My cousin Gina and gay cousin Terry were there. I arrived with Sharif. We had a massive long table in the middle of the room. Because my birthday is at the end of October everything is sort of getting a bit Christmassy and inside there were twinkling lights. We all ate sausage and mash, which I was really into at the time. Mum hired a magician, just like she always used to when I had parties when I was little. She'd also organised a karaoke machine and at the end everyone just went for it. Someone videotaped it and when I watch it now it reminds me of what a great night it was. It was totally unexpected, but I had a great time.

My twenty-first birthday was a real turning point for me. I felt I could confidently say to my family that I needed to go away and live on my own for a while. But it wasn't all fun, fun, fun.

If you need help, ask for it. Don't be afraid of looking silly. Once I got drunk and I woke up at my friend's house and I wanted to go home really badly but I didn't want to wake anyone up. I didn't want to get up and go out drinking again and planned to sneak out so I didn't look like a party pooper. I called up my friend and I whispered, 'I need to get a taxi, what's the name of that taxi company, Addison Lee?' She said: 'Kelly, it's Addison Lee.'

I argue like crazy with my mum – who doesn't? But she's also the person I am the closest to. When I first moved to London, even though she felt like I'd abandoned her, I felt like she'd abandoned me because she didn't move to London with me. But why would she? I had left – and I'd left to find some freedom.

I missed my family terribly when I was in London, but as I created my own little life, the horrible homesickness pain didn't feel so bad. The one thing I've never stopped missing though is climbing into bed with Mum and getting a hug, especially when I've not been feeling well. She always makes me feel so much better.

Sometimes Mum drives me crazy. She gets her friends in the UK to keep an eye on me and tell her what I'm up to. I know she's looking out for me. I know her worries come from a good place, but sometimes I find it so suffocating. I think she just needs to let me get on with my life. I think it's something you can only relate to if you're a parent.

Club Kitchen

The great thing about that first year in London was that I got to spend time with Mum when she came back to do the second series of *The X Factor*. We had all been so excited when Simon Cowell approached Mum to do the ITV show the previous year but at first we had all been pissed off with him. After my father's quad bike accident he had said it was a publicity stunt to sell copies of our single, 'Changes'. But he had made his peace with Mum when he appeared on her chatshow in America a few months later. He'd not realised just how serious Dad's accident had been at the time. Now he wanted Mum to be a judge on the show with him and the music manager, Louis Walsh.

At that point we didn't know a huge amount about *The X Factor* – we didn't have a clue how massive it would become. We were all pleased that Mum was going to get an opportunity to show a side of her personality that only we had seen. I wanted the world to know how great she was. Also, Mum is a well-respected music manager and to be a mentor was right up her street.

What was so strange about that show was that people suddenly thought they knew her really well. I could see why, she was in their living room every week and because that's a person's most comfortable place, they instantly felt a connection. She was great with the younger contestants too, and she wasn't afraid to give them a hug when it all got too much. I think she found it really hard picking who should go through. She didn't want to disappoint anyone or ruin their dreams.

Today people come up to Mum in the street and speak to her like she's their own mum. It's weird because my TV mum is only a part of what Mum's like. But I am proud that people like her.

Fierce

'*Today people come up to Mum*

in the street and speak to her like

she's their own mum.

It's weird because my TV mum

is only a part of what Mum's like.

But I am proud that people like her.'

The downside to it was that so many people felt they could make a judgement about her. I've lost count of the number of people who have come up to me and criticised her. People don't realise how much it hurts when people have a go at my mum.

My mum pisses on things; she's pissed on me, my dad – everyone. The scary thing is, I've started to do it. I was in a club in east London a few months after I'd moved back to England and I met a guy. He asked if he could get a lift back with me because his place was just before mine. When I said yes he took that as maybe I was going to go back to his place too. I did actually need to go back to his house because I had to pee really badly. When I walked into his flat he pushed himself on me. I pushed him off and said, 'What the fuck are you doing?' I ran into one of the bedrooms and when I came out he had completely passed out.

So I went into his lounge, pulled my knickers down and pissed on his carpet. I left and got in the car. How dare he think that he had the right to do that? What kind of message did I telepathically give him that it was OK to touch me?

You can thank Mum for that crazy behaviour.

While Mum was on *The X Factor* she started working with a publicist called Gary Farrow. He also represents Elton John and other celebrities. Mum arranged for me to meet him at

Fierce

Claridge's Hotel in London. It's really posh and a bit fancy. Mum sometimes stays there when she's working in central London.

I met Gary in one of the private rooms. When I walked in, he had laid out all the negative press cuttings about me from over the years. They were going back to the days when I'd not behaved properly and given people the wrong impression of me. There were a whole bunch of them all in front of me. He sat me down in front of the press cuttings and said – in his cockney geezer way, 'Do you really want people to say these things about you? Do you really want to be perceived like this?'

'No, no I don't.' I said.

He barked back. 'Well, listen to me.'

I have become more frightened of him than my own father. When Gary shouts, fuck me, he shouts, but he has played a massive part in helping me sort my shit out and making me the person I am today. I owe him for that. He has helped me work on myself. With Gary's guidance and with Mum as my manager, I started to get offered some really cool jobs. It was what I'd always wanted – to do stuff without my family. To be known as just Kelly Osbourne. I was up for trying everything. But even I wasn't prepared for just how well it would all go.

CHAPTER FIFTEEN

A TURNING POINT

Would I be interested in auditioning for Chicago?
I couldn't believe it.

I WAS asked to be a guest judge on the new Sky One show, *Project Catwalk*, hosted by Liz Hurley. It wasn't like other reality TV shows. The contestants had to have genuine talent. The premise of the show was to find a clothes designer. Each week the contestants were given a different theme and they had to design and make the garment before displaying it for the first time on the runway. The least popular was voted off. It was highly pressurised for the contestants. If you weren't talented, you couldn't be on. It absolutely amazed me what they were capable of doing – I was in awe. I loved being a guest judge; I love clothes. So when, after the first series, Liz decided she didn't want to do it any more and the producers of the show asked me if I wanted to present it, straight away I said, 'Fuck, yeah!' It was my dream job.

I really wanted TV-presenting experience. I had also been asked to be a host on the Channel 4 show, *Popworld*, with

Alexa Chung and Alex Zane. It launched their careers. But it was very time-consuming, for very little money. I would have had to spend most of the week and evenings working on the show, even though it was a weekly programme. If I was being honest, I didn't want to interview bands either. If I like a song, I like it. I don't want to over-intellectualise or dissect a song with questions like, 'What does this lyric mean to you?' It bores me. It really does.

But *Project Catwalk* was great. I made some really good friends on that show. I thought the designer Ben de Lisi was amazing. He was one of the judges and the contestants' mentor. He probably felt like I was stepping on his turf a bit when I joined the show. At times I got the impression he didn't like me for that reason. We never had words, but I thought he became a bit of a diva towards the end. But he probably thought the same thing about me too.

That show was a massive learning curve for me. It wasn't a case of me rocking up and reading the autocue and then going home. Because of my dyslexia, I had to memorise everything on cards. The show took three months to record and I was learning twenty-eight pages of text a day. It's funny how the brain compensates. I discovered from doing that show that I have a bloody good memory, which is a fucking good job. The show ran for two series. I was so sad when it came to an end in 2008, but I was also really proud. Shows come and go. But I look back on it as a really great experience.

Before *Project Catwalk*, back in 2006, I was also approached by Ginger Productions, who made Jack's show, *Adrenaline*

Fierce

Junkie, about a concept for a show they had come up with called *Turning Japanese*. It involved me going to live in Japan for four weeks and immersing myself in their culture. They thought I would be good for it and I thought, 'Yeah, cool.'

Mum's make-up artist Jude came with me, and I'm so grateful he did, because it was a lonely experience at times. Being in Japan is such an intense experience. Two days can feel like two months. I've never been anywhere in the world where I stood on a street among thousands of people going about their business and felt so incredibly lonely and isolated. Japanese culture is very specific. I felt very conscious I wasn't bowing at the right time or saying the right thing. Well, I knew I wasn't saying the right thing, I couldn't speak a word of Japanese and that was unbelievably tough.

The film *Lost in Translation*, which is about two people visiting Tokyo and sometimes feeling incredibly lost, is scarily accurate. The jet-lag was horrendous, so I would often wake up at 3 a.m. and sit for hours looking out over the sprawling skyscrapers. I couldn't use my mobile, I couldn't read the underground system, no one understood me – it was scary! I felt like I couldn't do anything for myself because I had to go through a translator for everything – even when I needed a new toothbrush. I have never felt more lonely in all my life.

The Osbournes was a really big show out there, but they had always known me for having pink hair. My hair was blonde when I went to Japan so they assumed I was a prostitute! People were literally asking me all the time, 'Are you a hooker?' I couldn't believe it.

I tried all these different jobs while I was out there, but my favourite was working at a sex hotel – maybe that's why people thought I was a fucking prostitute! It was a hotel where people booked the room by the hour so they could fuck. They all live with their mothers in Japan and the houses are so tiny that it's really unacceptable to bring someone back and sleep with them. So they brought women to the hotel and I'd check them in. Then they would ring down for room service and I would have to take it up. Nearly every single one ordered beer and a Pot Noodle! I get the beer, but a Pot Noodle after sex?

Being in Japan forced me to do a lot of soul-searching because, apart from Jude, there was no one else to talk. I learned that I'm not very good at being alone. I missed home so much and I ate my feelings. I would sit in my apartment and eat. I couldn't find anything to eat that was green and wasn't seaweed. I couldn't find a vegetable anywhere. I ate bowls of rice and two avocados every day.

I was proud of myself for sticking it out. I really was. It was the longest that I've been without any familiarity and it taught me that that can be a good thing sometimes.

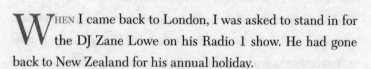

WHEN I came back to London, I was asked to stand in for the DJ Zane Lowe on his Radio 1 show. He had gone back to New Zealand for his annual holiday.

Just walking into that building in central London made my stomach flip over. I'd been there a few times to do interviews when we were over from America promoting *The Osbournes*, but actually presenting a show was just incredible.

I'd grown up on Radio 1. It reminded me of when I was in England, sitting in the back of my mum's car and looking at the clock as she drove us to school while wiping the Marmite and toast off my face. We were still only halfway to school and the heating wouldn't have kicked in yet in the car, but then I'd hear *Newsbeat* and a song that I wanted to hear and soon I'd forget how cold I was. Radio 1 played a big part in my growing up. To be able to work there was just fantastic.

After I'd covered for Zane, a load of people called in and said they liked the show I'd done. It was so cool. A few months later, the bosses at Radio 1 contacted me and said they were looking for a new DJ for their agony section on a Sunday night show called *The Surgery*. I was so fucking honoured to be asked.

The most daunting thing was doing the mixing desk, which is the panel of buttons in front of you that controls EVERYTHING! Every DJ has to do it. You should see the Radio 1 DJ Chris Moyles – he is very good at it. He's talking, fading songs in and out, reading the monitor for incoming emails, choosing his next song. I'm always mesmerised when I see him do his show.

I had lessons before I joined the show, but I was shit at the mixing desk. I really was. I would stand there with literally hundreds of knobs in front of me and two monitors at either side. I understood the basics and that was about it. I just about got by.

I saw it as a real privilege to offer advice to the people who contacted the station. I think I was a good person to do it because I'd been through a hell of a lot for someone so young.

I was twenty-three and I'd experienced drugs, rehab, cancer, death, tragedy . . . you name it.

On the back of the Radio 1 show I was offered my own agony aunt column in the *Sun* newspaper. It ran for several months and was really good fun. It's a popular newspaper and it was a big deal for me. I mean, I'm not a journalist. I didn't even finish high school, but all of a sudden I was writing for the *Sun*.

It wasn't easy doing the Radio 1 show. I often left feeling as if I had the weight of the world on my shoulders, especially if we'd had a lot of difficult calls that evening. It made me sad. At times it did feel like a lot of pressure, but we had a great team on the show and I always left knowing that we had given the best advice. I had made a pact with myself that I would never be patronising on that show. But I would be bloody honest. There are very few people out in the world who tell you how it really is. Working at the BBC and especially Radio 1, was really good fun, which just added to the whole experience.

But the show was also really tiring at times because it meant I was working seven days a week. A few months before I'd joined Radio 1 I'd been invited to New York to audition in front of the bosses of the hit musical *Chicago*.

One of my mum's contestants on *The X Factor*, Brenda Edwards, had starred in the musical and when Ashlee Simpson played the role of Roxie Hart in the show in London, Mum had gone to see her. So we sort of had connections.

Then one day, out of the blue, one of the bosses called Mum and asked her to see if I would be interested in auditioning for the show. I couldn't believe it. I can't dance to save my life.

'*I had made a pact with myself that I would never be patronising on that show. But I would be bloody honest. There are very few people out in the world who tell you how it really is.*'

A Turning Point

I went to audition in an empty theatre one afternoon during the summer and I was absolutely shitting myself. I sang 'Funny Honey', which is from the show and sung by the character Roxie Hart. When I finished, I was standing on the stage and everyone was just silent. I thought I must have fucked it up. But then someone piped up, 'Hell, you can sing.' I wasn't expecting that at all. I left not really knowing what to think and then we got a call asking if I would consider playing the role of Mama Morton. My instant reaction was, 'No way. I'm not playing a big mama. You want me to play that because I'm fat.' But after I'd calmed down I realised it would be a fucking cool role to play. I couldn't have played the Roxie role because there simply wasn't the time for me to learn the dance routines.

So I became the youngest person to ever play the role of Mama Morton and I was on stage for eight performances a week. I went into rehearsals in London at the end of August 2007, ready for my opening night on 10 September. The first day I walked into the theatre in Covent Garden I didn't feel like I belonged. I was surrounded by all these professional singers and dancers who sounded amazing and looked incredible. I was the name, sure, but I was on their turf now and I was so fucking nervous. They had worked their entire lives to get on that stage and I'd just been handed it. But the whole cast were all so lovely to me and they instantly tried to make me feel welcome.

On my opening night I had lots of mixed emotions – fear being the biggest. I'd not slept the night before so I was knackered too.

I'd invited all my family and my closest friends, which just made it even more nerve-racking.

I stood backstage and peeped behind the curtain watching everyone walk into the auditorium. Straight away I saw Amy Winehouse's beehive sticking up – you couldn't miss it! I couldn't believe the number of people who had come to support me. Especially when you think of all the dramas that go on between groups of friends. But they all came for me. Kate Moss came with Sharif and Fran Cutler and a whole bunch of other people. Mum, Dad, Louis Walsh, my half-brother and -sister Louis and Jessica and Dad's sisters were also there. Melinda had flown over from America to see it with my uncle Tony. I was shaking as I stood at the side of the stage, and just before I was about to go on and sing my solo, which was the song 'When You're Good to Mama', I threw up into my mouth and had to swallow it! Gross! I just remember walking on and seeing the biggest, brightest light shine on my face and my lonesome reflection on the stage next to me. And my heart was really pounding. I could hear it thudding inside me.

I can't remember actually singing my first song – not one bit. But when it was over, everyone clapping and cheering. It felt amazing – really amazing!

Mum and Dad came backstage to see me after the curtain had gone down. I was standing on my own on the stage waiting for them so we could have our picture taken for the newspapers. Dad's face appeared first from around the curtain at the side and he had tears streaming down his face. I cry when I think about it. He was so proud and he grabbed my hands and said! 'Pudding, I loved it. I really fucking loved it. You were so good, man.' Mum was crying too. They both just hugged me and I felt fantastic.

A Turning Point

'Chicago *was*

a massive discipline

for me; I was doing

eight shows a week.

It taught me a lot.'

It had been an emotional night for Mum. Her father had died a couple of months earlier and her brother had just sold a story about her to one of the newspapers. Plus her beloved dog Minnie had been taken ill in America the night before. I'd seen her the morning before the show and I'd asked her not to come because she was so upset – it had all got on top of her. But she did come and she got coaxed into doing the red carpet with my dad. It was a mistake because she broke down and burst into tears in front of the cameras.

At the time – I certainly don't feel that now – I was hurt by her actions and it felt like it took away everything I had worked for. The next day in the papers it was all about Mum. It was a night I had worked so fucking hard for and I wanted it to be about me.

I know that's selfish and mean. And I know they were proud of me, I got over it pretty quickly when I heard about the reviews. The next day I got a call from Caroline, my publicist, who works with Gary. She'd seen some of the reviews in the newspapers and they were all saying really great things. I just couldn't believe it, I really couldn't. When she was reading them out to me over the phone I was saying, 'Is this for real?' When she put the phone down, I dialled her number again and checked it wasn't a joke.

She was laughing and saying, 'No, I'm not joking! Now do you believe me that you were really good?'

It was another big turning-point for me. Theatre critics are known for being tough, but they were good to me and that meant a lot.

A Turning Point

The funny thing was that even though people were telling me I was good, I still just thought of myself as precocious, not talented, and also maybe a bit stupid because I was prepared to do all these crazy things people were offering me.

Chicago was a massive discipline for me; I was doing eight shows a week. It taught me a lot. Sometimes I was at the theatre all day – especially if a new cast member was joining and we had to rehearse with them. I could never eat before I went on because I was so nervous I would have thrown it up. The nerves never went away, so I'd have to wait until 11 p.m. before I could eat anything.

2007 was the best year of my life for so many reasons. It was the first time that I met Luke. One night after *Chicago*, I'd gone to the nightclub Bungalow 8 to see one of my friends who was DJ-ing. When I walked through the doors, the first person I saw was Luke. I turned to my friend Jenn, who used to be my PA, and said, 'Oh my God, he is so hot.'

Another friend overheard me and chipped in, 'That's Luke Worrall. He's on the cover of this month's *Dazed & Confused*. He is seventeen.'

At some point in the evening we got talking, but I thought he fancied another model, so I gave him my number and left. I thought, 'I am not going to try and pull a male model.'

For six months he got his friend to prank phone call me! I'd get random calls when no one would speak at the other end. It was really starting to piss me off.

Then the following March my neighbour, Kim Jones, was having a party and me and Luke were both invited. Kim Jones is the head designer for Dunhill – he is one of the funnest guys ever and I'm always hanging out at his house. When I heard that Luke was also going to the party I was really nervous. When we got chatting he told me he was twenty-three. I just smiled to myself and didn't say anything. I just said, "Oh, a year younger than me."

From that night we just clicked. The age thing has never been a problem for me. Where I'm lacking in maturity, he's not and vice versa. Our relationship worked from the beginning because he's the first person who's liked me as much as I've liked him and the other way around. We are always laughing and talking.

Luke is not afraid to be himself. He doesn't want to be the smartest person in the room, but he doesn't want to be the stupidest. He always speaks out when he doesn't get something. He's not afraid or self-conscious. To me, bravery is very attractive in a relationship.

Luke is the love of my life. When he proposed the following November, I said yes straight away. We're a little team and I couldn't imagine my life without him.

DURING my stint in *Chicago* I got a call from Caroline to say I had won an *Elle* Style Award for *Project Catwalk*. The category was Best Female TV. I cried. I couldn't believe it. This was an award that I had seen my peers and friends win. I'd

A Turning Point

given them out, but I'd never taken one home myself.

But then the nominations kept coming. I was nominated for an award for Best Takeover in a Role for *Chicago* from whatsonstage.com and then a Rising Star Award from the Sony Radio Academy Awards for my show on Radio 1. The last one was such a huge shock. I mean, they're the Oscars of the radio world. I couldn't believe it.

Just to be nominated for those awards was a big fucking deal for me, it really was. I had to leave the Sony Awards halfway through the night and jump into a cab to go to the *LK Today* High Street Fashion Awards. I'd been voted by the viewers of Lorraine Kelly's show as the Best Dressed Celebrity in High Street Fashion. I was thrilled because it was an award that had been voted for by the British public, which meant a lot. Getting these awards was incredible. All these great things were happening and it felt too good to be true.

I finished my stint in *Chicago* at the end of November 2007. It was earlier than I'd planned, but I'd hurt my back when I'd been given a night off to host the *National TV Awards* for ITV2 with Jack. The pain was so bad that I was in hospital for nearly two weeks. I was sad not to complete my time, but I was also proud that I'd stuck at it for as long as I was able and that I'd enjoyed it.

I got an extra boost when *Glamour* magazine called to say I had been shortlisted for Theatre Actress of the Year for my role in *Chicago* at their annual awards. They'd put a voting form for all the categories in an issue of their magazine before the awards in June and readers had to tick their winners and post the form back to the magazine. A month later, I got a call to say I had won the award. I cried – again! I had loved doing *Chicago*, so to get an award for my role was an extra bonus. It really meant something to me.

On the night of the event it was pissing it down. The event is always held in a marquee in Berkeley Square in central London. I was really nervous, but Claire from Mum's office and Anna, my friend and my PA at the time, were with me, along with the guys from Gary's office – Caroline and Claire – and Gary and his wife, Jane. Kimberley Stewart was on the table with a friend and Gordon Smart, who is a showbiz journalist from the *Sun* newspaper, was there too.

All my friends were there – Davinia Taylor, David Gardner and Jimmy B were on the table next to me. Jimmy was receiving an award on behalf of Kate Moss. Alexa Chung was on one of the other tables. The American singer Beth Ditto was also there – I just fucking love her. She really doesn't give a shit about what people think about her. She's as cool as fuck. The TV presenter and comedian Paul O'Grady was the host, which was great because he's a really good friend of Mum's and everyone in our family.

But I was still nervous. I can't really remember going up for the award, but everyone clapped, so I must have said all the right things!

A Turning Point

Afterwards, I just wanted to get the shit out of there. Not because it isn't a great party – because it always is – but I always feel so bloody self-conscious. Kate had organised celebratory drinks for me at her house, so Davinia, David Gardner, Jimmy and me went over and had such fun!

The next day I felt really proud because 2007 had been such an amazing year for me and to get all the recognition for jobs that I had done on my own just made it even better.

It made me think of a party I had been to with Mum a year earlier. It was a Christmas party organised by the jewellers Theo Fennell. I was on a table with Mum and a whole bunch of other people including the actor Hugh Grant, who was sitting next to me. He turned to me and said, 'I come to these things, and I, erm, I don't even know who you are. Are you on a reality TV show?'

I turned to face him and replied, 'Well I don't even know who you are, apart from that you fucked a prostitute.'

Everyone went silent – including his then girlfriend Jemima Khan – and Hugh just looked and me and in the most posh English accent ever, replied, 'You bitch!'

Mum burst out laughing and then he did! He kind of broke the ice. Later a woman came on the stage, took off all her clothes and smoked a cigarette out of her fanny. I swear to God. Everyone stopped eating their Christmas pudding. Well, it put them off.

But winning those awards and thinking about how a year earlier people thought I was some kid from a reality TV show made me realise how far I'd come.

I felt really proud. I really did.

CHAPTER SIXTEEN

FALLING IN LOVE WITH FASHION

'Kelly Osbourne, you're not going out wearing that!'

I DIDN'T give a shit about clothes when I was growing up. I wasn't like the other girls in my class, who would all gather around in the classroom and say dumb stuff like, 'Oh my God, I want the new Hello Kitty bag.'

You'd be more likely to hear me say, 'Where are my leggings, my wellies and my fleece so I can go and play in the garden.'

I had a few abstract, girly things like my jumper with bells on that made a tinkling sound when I jumped around. I had the odd pink jumper too, but you could definitely say I was a tomboy throughout my childhood.

My mum always bought our clothes for us. We went to a place called Wendy House near Welders in Beaconsfield. It's been there since the sixties and Jack and I would go with Mum in the car and pick out the things we liked.

I wore girly things when I had to. I loved my party dresses. I always used to have the best party dresses when I was at school because my mum used to buy them in America so no one else had the same one. They were really frilly and ridiculous. My mum has still got them all. But that was only because it was a special occasion. The rest of the time I couldn't have cared less about what I wore.

During the summer holidays, I'd wake up at Welders, go to one of the wardrobes that were on the landing outside mine, Jack and Aimee's bedrooms and pick out my scruffy jeans and a T-shirt. Jack would be doing the same and then we'd head out to the garden. My mum and dad wouldn't see us until tea-time.

As a kid, I don't think you should be worrying about wearing the latest designer stuff. Fuck me, you're going to spend so many of your adult years thinking about clothes and what you should wear that you need to give yourself a break when you're only seven years old!

WHEN we moved to America I was thirteen and I really wanted to fit in. I made my mum take me to the shop Fred Segal so I could buy a new outfit. I bought the baggiest jeans you've ever seen in your life, a pair of Vans trainers (they were the coolest thing to have at the time) and a T-shirt. I then bought this stupid wallet that I attached to a chain and I'd have it tucked in my pocket with the chain dangling out. I then insisted my mum buy me a skateboard. I didn't have a fucking clue how to ride it. Instead, I used to carry it under my arm everywhere I went because I thought it looked cool. I used to walk down Sunset with this bloody skateboard sitting under my arm – I must have looked such an idiot. But I didn't care. When we'd first arrived in LA, I'd noticed a lot of kids my age were wearing the same thing, so I wanted to fit in. I really did.

I was permanently hanging around with boys – either Jack, Uncle Tony, my dad or the guys at Ozzfest – and I was really influenced by them. The last thing I wanted to do was rock up at one of my dad's concerts in some ridiculously frilly dress looking all prissy. They would have spent the whole time taking the piss out of me. I did have this red and white polka dot dress from a store called The Limited in the Beverly Center. That was about as girly as I got in terms of fashion. There was one summer that I lived in that dress. I still have it.

A massive fashion turning-point for me came when I watched the film *Clueless*. It starred Alicia Silverstone and was set in a high school in Beverly Hills. Alicia's character, Cher, was mega-rich and wore really expensive designer clothes. When it first came out I was only eleven and sort of growing out of my tomboy stage. When we moved to America, I watched it again and it had a major influence on me. Not in the sense that I wanted to wear the clothes she did, but it got me thinking about how what you wear can help you make a statement about how you feel.

When we were filming *The Osbournes* I was going through a typical 'my life is so bad' phase. So I experimented with lots of different looks. I was always wanting to show my mum how pissed off I was by wearing the most outrageous thing, like a ripped shirt or a short skirt. Nearly every time I went out my

Falling In Love With Fashion

mum would be screaming at me as I was walking out of the door, 'Kelly Osbourne, you're not going out wearing that!' I never used to listen.

I was dying my hair every colour under the sun. I cringe when I look back at pictures of me from then. Unlike most people, who can shove their embarrassing pictures to the back of a drawer, I am faced with mine every time a magazine wants to do a piece on 'how Kelly Osbourne was a chubby teenager'. I know I fucking was! I don't need to be reminded every week.

I once wore this yellow T-shirt saying 'Young, willing and eager' with a mini skirt with a bow on the side at an MTV event. I had my hair brushed over my eye and I was giving the finger to the camera. I thought I fucking rocked. I didn't. God knows what I was thinking.

My mum is a shopaholic – she just can't stop herself. But she has had a massive influence on my style over the years from just being around her clothes and reading her style books. She's always bought items from classic designers like Dior, Chanel and Versace. At Welders, my mum has a room full of clothes from the seventies, eighties and nineties. I'm always going through her rails and borrowing stuff. She has a great blue suit jacket by Versace that I wear all the time. We call it 'Sharon Osbourne Oxfam'. My mum has always had these great designers in her life and I get a lot of ideas from her.

On rainy afternoons at Welders I used to flick through my mum's Vidal Sassoon books from the sixties. I used to pick out my favourite hairstyles and the outfits the models were wearing.

I get a lot of my ideas for outfits from watching classic

Fierce

'Unlike most people, who can

shove their embarrassing pictures

to the back of a drawer,

I am faced with mine every time a

magazine wants to do a piece on "how

Kelly Osbourne was a chubby

teenager".'

American movies. I think the costumes of actresses like Bette Davis and Doris Day are just amazing. I kind of make a mental note and the next time I'm out, I'll look for something in a similar style.

I was fifteen the first time I went into the designer Vivienne Westwood's shop, just off Regent Street in central London. My mum was getting a dress made. I liked Vivienne before I knew exactly what she did. I fell in love with her for the way she looked. She wears what she wants to wear. That day in the shop, as my mum had her fitting, I tried on one of the dresses from the rail and it fitted me perfectly. I thought it looked amazing. Vivienne's clothes are made for women with a figure and her designs accentuate the hips and waist. But at the same time they have such edge. Over the years, she has lent me so many dresses to wear at premieres and parties. She has fitted me for clothes too, which has always been such a privilege.

When David and Victoria Beckham held their World Cup Party, Full-length and Fabulous, Vivienne came up to me and said, 'I don't know who you are, but I think I know your ma.' I'd met her loads of times – she'd fitted me for clothes. I thought it was hilarious that she didn't remember me.

As I've got older, I've fallen more and more in love with fashion and clothes. Meeting all these designers and them liking me is like a dream come true for me. I think about it all the time. I don't know how it's happened.

I was sitting in a restaurant in New York once and the designer Betsey Johnson was having dinner at a neighbouring table. The waiter came over with a message from Betsey written in lipstick on a napkin. It said, 'Call me, babe.' I did, and from that day she's lent me clothes to wear.

I'm so very, very fortunate to have met so many great designers. I never take it for granted. I don't see myself as a model or a clothes horse, so for a world-renowned designer to want me to wear their clothes is just amazing.

Alexander McQueen has become a really good friend of mine over the years. We met when I first moved to London. There is something so very special about his clothes. Usually, it's not just a dress. It's a dress that you put on and it changes colour with your body temperature. Or he'll design a jacket that, when you take a picture, looks completely different to the naked eye.

In December 2007, I was doing press for my final series of *Project Catwalk*. During one shoot I got an email on my Blackberry from Karl Lagerfeld, who is a designer I'd loved for so many years. He loves photography too and often shoots for magazines. He asked if he could shoot me for the magazine *Purple*. I couldn't fucking believe that he wanted me to do it. I replied, 'Hell, yeah.'

Karl is the coolest and most influential person in fashion. For him to even know that I existed was just incredible. My friend Christopher had given Karl my email address when he'd asked him about me. It was the stuff of dreams. Really it was.

I went to meet Karl at Brown's Hotel, which is really quite fancy, in Mayfair, London. I walked in and there were all these super-tall and super-skinny models getting fitted for a fashion show. They put me in a room with them and they all turned and looked at me as if to say, 'What the fuck is she doing here?'

I couldn't believe how thin they all were. I thought to myself, 'Oh, please. Go and eat some cotton wool balls.' (Apparently models eat cotton wool soaked in orange juice when they're really hungry. It's fucking ridiculous.)

But being with them all just made me even more self-conscious and then I started to think, 'What the fuck am I doing here?

The hotel does these really spicy mojitos, so I had one for courage and I felt so much better.

The whole experience was like something from the movie *The Devil Wears Prada*. I stood in the suite surrounded by the most amazing clothes and Karl came over and kissed me on each cheek – it was incredible. It was so unbelievably cool. He started showing me all these picture clippings of ideas for the shoot. He had come up with the idea of a mademoiselle in the progression of a nervous breakdown. I started off looking quite demure, but by the end my lipstick was smeared all over my face and my hair was tangled and I was scrunched up in an armchair. The whole experience was liberating. I just went with what he told me to do and it created a set of pictures I'll never do again. It was a truly great experience.

I'm in a very fortune position in that I can afford to buy designer clothes, but I never take that fact for granted. I once spent eight thousand dollars on an Oscar de la Renta dress. I've worn it a few times. I wore it for one of Elton John's White Tie and Tiara parties. I really thought long and hard about buying it, but I knew that I would have it for the rest of my life. I think when it became fashionable to wear vintage clothing again, it made me realise that if I kept the expensive items I'd bought and sold them in ten years' time – or even longer – I'd be able to make money from them. My clothes have become an investment.

I'm addicted to buying shoes. I've got about a thousand pairs. The collection is probably worth a ridiculous amount – I couldn't even begin to start totting it up. I think it might frighten me. My favourite shoes in the whole world are my 'Gina Sparkles'. I first started wearing them in 2005 when they had quite a thick heel, before they became thinner. They're a stiletto shoe with a sparkly effect in different colours. When I went into the musical *Chicago* they made a pair for me with the thick heel so I could wear them on stage as I did a lot of standing during the performance. They've been making them for me ever since. I can't believe they make them for me. I still get excited when they do and I never take it for granted. Designers have lent me clothes before they've gone on the runway and that's just amazing.

CHAPTER SEVENTEEN

MY BIGGEST LESSON

With anything else in your life, like your job, you may have a good day or a bad day. But there is none of that with addiction. You have to fight all the time.

A COUPLE of weeks before my twenty-fourth birthday, I was running around my house in London trying to get all my shit together for my move back to America. We were due to start filming our family variety show *The Osbournes: Reloaded* at the end of October 2008 and it meant I would be moving back to LA for the first time since I'd relocated to London three years earlier.

At first I was sceptical about doing another show with my family. Apart from presenting the Brit Awards in London earlier in the year, in February, it had been six years since we'd worked together on *The Osbournes*. A lot had happened since then.

Going back and being the predictable 'big-mouth daughter' again didn't really appeal to me. I'd grown up and that person really wasn't me any more. Of course it wasn't. I was just a teenager when I'd been on that show.

I wanted to show people that person wasn't me any more and I knew it would be great fun to work with Mum, Dad and Jack, so I said yes. I think Jack felt the same reluctance. We both knew there would be the usual family dramas; he said/she said bollocks. But that was never going to change.

Mum was organising it all and it was going to be shown on the American TV network, Fox. It meant that I would have to move back to my house in West Hollywood for at least three months while we filmed at a studio nearby, as well as doing some filming across America.

That afternoon, when I was trying to do all my last-minute packing, I turned to my housemate, who'd walked into my bedroom, and said, 'If I go back to LA I know what is going to happen to me.' I just knew and I felt like I had to tell someone what I was thinking. I just blurted it out. It had been on my mind.

There was no IF. I was booked on that plane and I was going. I was worried. Those feelings of anxiety that I'd had when I'd been growing up in LA were starting to come back. I never feel good about myself when I'm in LA. I don't feel good enough or socially accepted.

I'd been living in London for three years by then and I'd built up my own little life and I was worried about what would happen and how I'd feel when I moved back to America.

I'm not going to lie, since my last visit to rehab just before my twenty-first birthday, I'd not been completely clean. I'd relapsed. I'd often turned to painkillers to block out a stressful situation. They'd not been massive falls and I'd been able to get myself back on track with the help of my family and friends. I felt happy in London, so that was always a help.

The thing is, when you're an addict, you're an addict. I can't even have the cold and flu medication Night Nurse because I would become addicted to it. I have been on and off painkillers since I was sixteen. In January 2008, I relapsed and started taking painkillers, but they actually made me sick. I was sick for five hours solid. I thought maybe I'd cracked it, but I hadn't.

Addiction is addiction. If you are addicted to shopping, you could be addicted to drugs. If you are addicted to counting the number of stairs you climb, you could be addicted to drugs. Lots of people swap one drug for another. I think maybe I thought I could manage taking drugs and then not taking drugs. But it doesn't really work like that. Addiction takes over everything in your life. You don't think, 'Oh I'll just get this job done and then I'll take drugs.' You take whatever, whenever!

What really upsets me is the prejudices people have towards drug addicts. I've seen this happen a few times in LA and it drives me crazy. Some well-dressed person will be walking down the street and they'll literally recoil at the sight of a drug-addicted homeless person on the street. Or they'll mutter 'drug addict' under their breath. But you know what? That judgemental person probably doesn't think twice about the number of painkillers they've got at home or the fact they take them – and a few more than they should – just to get them through a difficult patch. Well, that makes them a drug addict too. Just because they're living in a mansion in Beverly Hills and that person is sleeping on the streets makes no difference whatsoever.

My Biggest Lesson

'*Addiction is addiction.*

If you are addicted to shopping, you could

be addicted to drugs. If you are addicted

to counting the number of stairs you climb,

you could be addicted to drugs.

Lots of people swap one drug for another.'

So, knowing how hard it was to fight my addictions every day meant that I had the 'fear' I would relapse again if I went to America.

During the time I have relapsed, it's often been because someone has thought I've been taking drugs, but I haven't. So instead of thinking, 'Well, I know best.' I think to myself, 'Well, if they suspect I'm taking drugs, I might as well.'

I landed back in LA in the October. Don't for one minute think that I'm not grateful or thankful for my life there. I know I'm very lucky. All my family are there and I have a lovely house. The front looks out across the Hollywood hills and it has a really nice garden at the back, which is private and a suntrap. Although I don't go in the sun. That's probably another reason why I don't like LA.

In the morning the sun shines through into the kitchen, which is white with wooden beams. In the lounge it's full of family photographs and my favourite framed black-and-white picture of a wedding. I don't know who the couple are, I just liked the picture and bought it.

At first it was great to be back. The production meetings were fun and I got to see Mum, Dad and Jack all the time. But I soon began to feel anxious, bored, lonely and fucking uncomfortable.

I'm not into what people are into in LA. I'm not hungry for what they're hungry for – like fame.

Actually, it's more than that. I don't care if I have a tan or not. I couldn't give a shit if I go to the right dentist. I don't care. As long as my teeth are not hurting, I'm not going to sign up to a six-month waiting list to see some doctor who does a show on *E!*

that everyone is talking about and MUST go to. I won't do that shit. People go about things in a different way in LA.

The other big problem was that I was completely out of my old social circle. I've got friends there, but not like when I lived there. I left when I was twenty and, even though it had been little more than three years, they're life-changing years. I didn't fit in any more.

Girls in LA have a different routine; they wake up at 2 p.m. and their biggest decision of the day is what outfit they are going to wear to lunch at Fred Segal. I find that all so boring!

When I'm in London, I get up, put a massive coat over my pyjamas, roll up the bottoms so you can't see them and put on my UGG boots. I then walk to my little row of shops. I know everyone there. I know all the staff in Tesco, the ladies in the florist's and the butcher. I go and find them all and we have a chat. I buy the papers and then I walk back to my house. There, I feel like I'm part of a community.

In LA there is no interaction. Everyone gets in their big cars, drives to the supermarket or the mall, gets out, does their shopping, gets back in the car and goes home again. Or they'll get in their car, go to the gym and come home. Or they'll fucking get in their car, go to their plastic surgeon for some Botox and then come home.

There's very much a culture in LA – especially when you're the child of a celebrity – that is, 'I'm famous give me a show.' Meanwhile, I just think to myself, 'I'm another celebrity's daughter, why bother?' I don't feel like that in London though. I'm proud of the work I've done there. I'm proud of the jobs I've had.

We started recording the show at the beginning of the November, which was a mixture of doing stuff in front of a live audience and travelling around America. We did this sketch where we met other Osbourne families and Dad and I went to work in a drive-thru which was hilarious. Dad started throwing fries at people when they got to the window to collect their takeaway.

I thought it was a big risk doing the show, but I was glad to be doing it. It was scary at times because we didn't know what the public reaction would be. I was out of my comfort zone. I was away from my boyfriend Luke and my best friends. Luke was visiting as often as he could, but he had work commitments too. Everything that had been my life in London – that I had fought so hard for – felt like it was slipping away.

And so the only thing I felt like I had control of was whether I got high again. I didn't start using straight away. I was trying to fight it for a long time. At the beginning, I would take painkillers, but I could function. I'd take a couple to take the edge off feeling anxious after we'd finished recording. But like with any addiction, my body started to crave more and more pills to get the same effect. It became ridiculous and I was soon back on the phone to my dealer again.

Even I wasn't prepared for the speed of my downward spiral. It was that quick, it just completely took over. Addiction can be a slow or quick progression. For me, when I was in LA, it was very quick and very painful, and it was so scary. We were having a break from filming the show in the middle of December and I wasn't leaving the house, I was living in my

My Biggest Lesson

Drug addiction is a tough place
to be in – it's not fun

bedroom. I was not showering, I was not brushing my teeth and the only relationship I had was with the pizza delivery man. I'd get up, open the door, take the pizza and go back into my bedroom. People probably thought I was fucking dating him. I wasn't. I just couldn't be bothered to do anything other than pick up the phone and order food, which was easy.

The only other time I was getting up was to take more drugs so I could fall back to sleep again. I was trying to block everything out.

I'm not a social user – I never have been. I'm not one of those people who walks into a club and starts handing out pills like they're penny sweets from a goody bag to everyone around me. My addiction is a very lonely and miserable place. I isolate myself. And that's exactly what I was doing. I was completely isolating myself from everyone who loved and cared about me. Drug addiction isn't always about snorting cocaine or taking an Ecstasy tablet before you walk into a nightclub, having a great night and then getting up for work the next morning. Drug addiction is a tough place to be in – it's not fun.

WE were due in the studio one day to finish bits of recording. It was a massive struggle for me to get in and it was the first time I'd used while we were filming. But I needed to take something because I'd been spending all day at home.

We were only meant to have been in the studio for half an hour, but it dragged on. One minute I was sitting in a chair on stage, the next minute I'd nodded off. I'd literally fallen asleep in front of everyone – my family and the production crew. I woke up and they were all just looking at me.

I didn't bother to come up with an excuse. I had lied so much and I was so fed up with myself that I just knew I had to get some help. I'd become so egotistical again and I didn't like the person that the drugs were turning me into. I hated everyone. I was so angry at myself. I didn't want to admit it and I felt such shame. The thing that frightened me the most was how quick my downfall was. I'd started using mid-December and I was on my way to rehab on 19 January.

I spoke to my mum. I knew it was the right thing to do. The fact that I didn't die during that month is a miracle. It was like I was suicidal. I wasn't sitting there with my pink Venus razor blade, holding it to my wrist. That isn't me. But it was more like I was taking enough pills to kill any human being. I was waking up in the morning and tapping my body to check it was all there. I simply couldn't believe I'd survived. But because I'd built up such a tolerance I had been lucky. I had been really, really lucky. Don't think I don't know that.

AFTER the incident in the studio, I had a chat with my mum and dad. The next day, a really lovely woman from the Hazelden Alcohol and Drug Rehabilitation Center in Newberg, Oregon, came to collect me. I didn't know what I was packing. At that point I just wanted to fall asleep and not wake up.

In my head I was thinking, 'I can't believe I have to deal with this again.' We had to get on a plane to fly to the centre and I was just sitting there feeling like absolute shit.

I couldn't believe that I was going to have to go around and tell everyone, 'Yeah I'm OK now, but I fucked up – again.' It felt like my life had been *Groundhog Day* since I was sixteen.

I knew I was about to learn more about myself. That was the positive thing and it was what I was trying to concentrate on as I sat on the plane.

ANNOYED doesn't even come near to how I felt when I walked into Hazelden that afternoon though. It is tucked away in the countryside – a white building that sits in twenty-three acres of secluded land. It's surrounded by fir trees and if it wasn't for the fact it's a rehab facility, it would be a nice place to go on holiday.

I felt sheer and utter self-hate and disappointment knowing that the only reason I was walking in there was because something I had done sucked. It really, really sucked. For the first two days I had to undergo a medical detox. They took all my possessions off

Fierce

me – all I had was the pyjamas I was wearing. I was in a room that had two beds, a bathroom and a TV. I was on my own in there for three days. I only ever saw another person when someone came in every two hours to check my blood pressure, check that I was taking the medicine they had given me to take off the edge off my detox and make sure I was drinking fluids.

I hated it. I was lying on my bed and I couldn't move. I was throwing up, shaking and sweating. My bones were shaking, I was in such a bad way. It was horrible. I felt horrible. The night sweats were the worst. I couldn't stop shaking and I was literally soaking wet as the drugs left my system.

AFTER three days they gave me my luggage back and I was allowed to have a shower. It was so good to get out of those pyjamas. I was then moved to room which I shared with another patient. From the moment I opened my eyes in the morning, the doctors and nurses kept me busy. I'd get up, do my medication, and then I would shower, have breakfast, a meeting, lunch, then another meeting. It was the same for everyone in there.

The women were segregated from the men. If you even talked to a man you would be kicked out. That wasn't a problem for me. I didn't want to talk to anyone. Some of the people in there were being treated for sex addiction, so we had to be mindful of what we wore and keep covered up. But who wants to go into rehab and dress like a slut? I don't fucking get it. But some of the women were like, 'I want to wear this tube top and I don't care.' I couldn't understand who they were trying to look sexy for. They were in rehab, for fuck's sake.

271

My Biggest Lesson

In the first week, I'd wake up every day and I would see the newspapers laid out on the side and there would be an article on me and how I was a drug addict. People wanted to read newspapers in there. They couldn't make exceptions for me – why should they? Catching the headlines was horrendous though. It was a massive reality-check and it made it so much harder for me. I'd expected the papers to write about it – I wasn't being precious. I was the one who had gone into rehab. Going into a facility is humiliating enough without having a whole bunch of people remind you every day. But there was nothing I could do.

In that first week I could speak to people outside, so I called Luke. It was lovely to hear his voice. In the last week, I had family therapy and Mum, Dad and Luke came. Seeing them and having them there really helped me.

My mum has had major issues with admitting that I am a drug addict. Also, this was the first time that my parents had ever come to the family therapy sessions that you have when you're in rehab. They had never wanted to do them before in the way that the institution wanted them to. In many ways, I can understand why. There had been times in the past when Mum couldn't come because she had prior work commitments. I understood that she couldn't just drop everything because I had suddenly decided I needed help, even though she had been trying to help me for years.

The thing that got me, though, was when they had refused to do the family sessions. Mum said she didn't want us airing our dirty laundry in front of people. There was me sitting there thinking, 'We did a reality TV show!'

But this time Mum and Dad came and it really, really helped.

My dad feels terribly guilty about the fact that I am addicted to painkillers. He feels like it's his fault that I am a drug addict because he's a drug addict too. My mum also feels terribly guilty. She feels that she wasn't a good parent and she let me down. She blames herself and says it's her fault.

Do you have any idea how that makes me feel? It absolutely breaks my heart that my parents feel that way. It really does, and there is nothing I can do about it, and I think about it all the time. I can't help it. My mum and dad shouldn't feel that way. They really shouldn't. What they're thinking and saying simply isn't true. My mum taught me right from wrong. I knew exactly what I was doing and there was nothing she could have done to have stopped me.

I was sixteen and old enough to know better. No one forced me to take them. They didn't shove them in my mouth. I could make my own mind up. I'd also seen what my dad was like when I was growing up and so I knew better than anyone what drugs could do to individuals and families.

It was my choice and I took them.

I blame myself.

AFTER thirty days, I left rehab and flew back to be with my family in LA. I felt relieved that I had done it and that I no longer felt the pain I'd been suffering before I'd gone in. And, for the first time, I felt very hopeful. I knew that I had been given another chance at my life, at my career – at happiness. I wanted to grab it.

'I felt relieved that I had done it and that I no longer felt the pain I'd been suffering before I'd gone in.

And, for the first time, I felt very hopeful. I knew that I had been given another chance at my life, at my career – at happiness. I wanted to grab it. '

If I think about relapsing again, it makes me want to cry. I worry about it, but I'm realistic. For the first time since I started taking painkillers when I was sixteen, I feel like I've learned my biggest lesson: there is a strong chance I will relapse. But because I recognise that, I almost feel like I've got the strength to fight it.

I think I was too caught up in pretending that I could be clean for ever before and that just put more pressure on me. I suppose I was in denial a lot of the time. Addiction doesn't take a day off. With anything else in your life, like your job, you may have a good day or a bad day. But there is none of that with addiction. You have to fight it all the time. Now that I know that, I don't feel so scared. I'm trying to put the right plans in place.

I wish. I wish with every fibre of my being. I really wish, more than anything that it was just as simple as me deciding that I don't want to do drugs any more. If that was the case, I wouldn't take them again. But it isn't. It really isn't.

For a normal person, that's what they do – when they don't want to do something any more, they stop doing it. But when you're an addict, you can't. I wish to God I could.

As much as I wish I didn't relapse, as much as I wish I didn't fall off the wagon, every time I relapse it's that little bit more embarrassing. I have to pick myself up and have everyone know I'm back in the same position again. But I'll fight it. I really will.

My Biggest Lesson

CHAPTER EIGHTEEN

DANCING WITH THE STARS

I'd had stage fright before, but this time it was different. It was more than just feeling sick – being out on that dance floor made me feel naked.

*D*ANCING WITH THE STARS is the American version of *Strictly Come Dancing* in the UK. It's massive – and easily gets over twenty million viewers some weeks. Ever since it first aired on the channel ABC in 2005, my mum's office had received email from the producers asking if I would take part.

If I'm honest, when I had seen the show, I'd always thought to myself, 'Ugh, a show about stupid dancing.' But really I was thinking, 'God I would love to be able to dance'. I can't dance for shit. One of the reasons I didn't push for the role of Roxie in the musical *Chicago* was because there simply wasn't the time for me to learn the dance routines. Those moves wouldn't have come naturally, put it that way.

Dancing with the Stars is shown twice a year, so in April 2009, the email, once again, came through asking me to take part in the show airing in September. I know this sounds pretty dumb, but this time I was interested. And that was purely because the email didn't come via my mother's office, but directly to me, instead. It felt like it was my idea, so I signed up. That's just me being stupid because this had actually been the first time I was free to do it because I'd always had other commitments. Call it what you want, it was probably bloody good timing more than anything.

SINCE coming out of rehab in February 2009, I'd been pretty low key. I'd stayed in my house in the Hollywood Hills so I could be near my family, and when he wasn't working, Luke would be with me.

There was the predictable 'first picture of Kelly Osbourne out of rehab' in the papers when I had been shopping in Malibu with my Mum. So, I wanted to do *Dancing with the Stars* because I thought it would give me a confidence boost.

And, I'd be lying if I didn't admit that I wanted to do the show to lose a bit of weight. In the months after I'd left rehab, I'd got bigger – that wasn't a major problem because I was getting better. But because I was by now feeling stronger, I wanted to do something that would help get me a bit thinner.

To say I was shitting myself about the whole experience was an understatement – I was so unbelievably nervous. I was completely out of my comfort zone.

'*The whole* **Dancing with the Stars** *thing went on to become such an emotional experience for me* – *I literally* lived and breathed *that show for four months.*

And I pretty quickly learnt that if I didn't put everything into it, *if I didn't play the game*, if I stopped trying,

then I didn't do well'

My dance partner was unveiled about two months after I'd signed up. He came to meet me one afternoon when I was at my mum and dad's house in LA. The first time I met Louis van Amstel I just felt relief because I knew he was older than me and wouldn't take any crap. If I'd had someone the same age as me, I'd have wrapped them around my little finger and got away with murder. Louis was definitely the boss from day one.

After that first meeting, we drove to a dance studio in LA and I thought I would learn a whole new dance. But instead Louis spent three hours teaching me how to walk properly. I didn't realise there was a problem with my walking! Eventually, I learned my first dance – the Viennese waltz. I started off training for three hours a day – by the end I was doing at least six hours a day and some days could be as long as fourteen hours. That show gets you like that.

We filmed the show's opening sequence weeks before the show aired which is when I met the other sixteen contestants. I didn't really know them well, but I'd met the singer Donny Osmond before when we filmed a Pepsi advert together and I'd heard of Mya, who is an American singer.

By the time the first show came round on 21 September 2009, I was sick with nerves. You don't just rock up minutes before and do your stuff on stage. The show is recorded at CBS Studios (even though it airs on ABC) in Los Angeles – right next to where they film American Idol – and I'd be there from 8am rehearsing before the show went out live at 8pm, so the pre-show build up was huge. I'd had stage fright before, but this

Fierce

time it was different. It was more than just feeling sick – being out on that dance floor made me feel naked.

My mum and dad were in the audience that first night. And, when I finished the routine, I just burst into tears and ran over to them. I couldn't believe that I'd actually done it. One of the judges, Len Goodman, who is also a judge on *Strictly Come Dancing* in the UK, said, 'It was the best Viennese Waltz of the night.' It was like a dream – we got 23/30 making us second on the leader board.

The whole *Dancing with the Stars* thing went on to become such an emotional experience for me – I literally lived and breathed that show for four months. And I pretty quickly learnt that if I didn't put everything into it, if I didn't play the game, if I stopped trying, then I didn't do well. Every day for ten weeks, I'd wake up, take a shower, drive to the dance studio, practise, practise, practise and drive home to bed.

When Louis and I made the final on the 24 November – I seriously couldn't believe it. Was I excited? Fuck yeah. One of the biggest regrets of that final week was falling over during my performance. When we did the dress rehearsal – as we had every week – I'd not worn the body make-up. It's called body gleam and it's like baby oil. When we performed for real – me glistening like fuck – Louis picked me up and I slipped out of his hands and straight onto the floor. But I laughed it off – I just wanted to have fun and enjoy my last time on the dance floor.

The whole *Dancing with the Stars* thing was such a massive journey for me and I know so many people say that bullshit, but it really was. It represented more than just a dance contest. It was the first thing I had attempted since coming out of rehab and it was great fun, and I did well – I was so happy when I came third. When I'd first started, I'd not thought I'd make it past the third week let alone the tenth!

But, I guess the best thing about the show was how much people seemed to love it. People would literally stop me in the street and tell me how much they were enjoying it. You know what it is, people automatically expect me to shout my mouth off and say something obnoxious because in the past, I have been like that. But instead, I showed emotion when I was on *Dancing with the Stars*, and was honest and I think people found that surprising.

So, I'd gone on the show in the hope that I would lose some weight. But all that got kind of forgotten when I stepped into the dance room for the first time. All I became concerned about was learning – and remembering – the dance steps so I didn't screw up on the live shows.

But, with every week that went by, I realised my body was changing. *Dancing with the Stars* was the harsh realisation that there is no quick fix. For years now people have been telling me that in order to lose weight, you need to eat less and exercise more. That's exactly what I was doing and the weight kept dropping off.

Of course I knew I was losing weight, but it didn't really hit me until February 2010 when a friend sent me an email saying,

Fierce

'Kelly look at you now compared to how you were this time last year.' And I was like, 'Yeah thanks – but shit, you're right.' I was a US size 2 and I'd lost 50lbs. I figured that if *Dancing with the Stars* had got me this far, I was going to continue.

Y<small>OU</small> know the thing that pissed me off the most when I lost the weight? It was all the people who came out of the woodwork and suddenly wanted to work with me because I wasn't 'fat Kelly Osbourne' anymore. That became glaringly obvious when I attended New York Fashion Week in February 2010. I was going because I'd been invited by the designer Betsey Johnson, who asked me to walk in the show for her Fall 2010 collection. It was an honour. I've known Betsey for years – every since she sent me a message on a napkin with her number on when we were both dining in the same New York restaurant. I was sixteen and she was the first designer to lend me clothes. Over the years, whether I was fat or thin, Betsey continued to send me clothes and I loved her for it. She didn't discriminate.

Doing the show was great fun – I really didn't mind taking the piss out of myself. For fuck's sake, I walked down that catwalk wearing a stick-on moustache at one point.

But, you'd have thought that I'd have felt a sense of satisfaction walking down that runway. But it was bittersweet. There in the crowd were all the people, who in the past had called me fat and ugly. It's hard not to build resentment when you have a whole bunch of people in front of you being really nice just because I've lost weight. All the people who'd had digs at me, never wanted to lend me clothes, never wanted to help me out. But suddenly, they were all chucking stuff at me, telling me how great I looked and offering to give me this that and the other. For the record, their opinions mean absolutely nothing to me now – but back then, those criticisms affected me much more deeply than I could have comprehended.

Chucking out all my clothes and buying new ones has become the fun part. I definitely don't want to go back to being the size I was before I did *Dancing with the Stars*. But I don't think being skinny is something that is natural to me. I will always have to keep an eye on it. I wish I could say there was a big old secret to my weightloss, but there isn't. I don't deny myself anything – I just have smaller portions and I don't eat nasty junk food. But it doesn't matter whether I'm fat or thin, my personality is still the same. That's what counts.

ADVICE

From addiction to awards and fashion faux pas to first night nerves, I've always been making mistakes and learning from them. I hope that the embarrassing stories I've shared with you can help you avoid one or two of your own!

I do want to help other people make the right decisions with the difficult choices we all face when growing up. So, I've gone out and got the best advice I can find from people I love, respect and always listen to. I've included Louis Walsh's advice on making it in the music industry, tips from Neil, my sought-after make-up artist at MAC and many others. And for when things get really serious I've gone to the organisations that really can help. I hope you find this section useful.

DEALING WITH YOUR FAMILY

ONE of the biggest lessons I've learned as I've got older is that parents and people who care about us often protect us from things, because they know something we don't. You might wonder why they didn't tell you something. You might be bloody annoyed they didn't tell you something; but nine times out of ten there is a good reason why.

It could be something obvious, but most of the time I think parents protect us because their life experience tells them it's best that we don't know. Coming to accept that there are things we don't know can be really tough, but being in any relationship – with your family, a friend or a partner – means trusting the other person, and that includes letting them not tell you things if they think that's the best thing to do.

Whatever you're struggling with, whether it's an addict in the family or you're worried about your mum or dad for other reasons, there's a completely fantastic organisation called the Samaritans who are always there to talk through the tough times. They're completely confidential, they're at the other end of the phone and they'll listen to you, whatever the problem.

Samaritans offers a twenty-four-hour confidential emotional support service for anyone in the UK and Ireland. You can call their volunteers, email or write for advice or go to one of the 202 branches and talk face to face.

Chris
Po Box 9090
Stirling
FK8 2SA

☎ 08457 90 90 90
✉ jo@samaritans.org

Y<small>OU'RE</small> going to argue with your brother or sister. That's an absolute definite. Over the years I've had so many arguments with my siblings. The fact is you're spending every day with them, so of course they're going to piss you off every so often.

When things got bad between me and my brother, Mum would sit us both down and try and talk it through. It actually really helped that we were able to put across our own points of view. You should suggest this to your parents if arguments get out of hand. Remember that your brother or sister loves you, the same way you love them. It doesn't matter how hard things get, you should always remind each other of that. Your family should be the most precious thing in your life. When times get really shitty, they're always there for you and always will be.

If you're going through a patch where you just can't get along with each other there are other people who you can turn to though. Check out Teensay: they provide advice and articles on relationships and many other subjects. You can contact the online agony aunt with any questions or issues you may have and you can swap stories in the chatrooms and forums. www.teensay.co.uk/life

I<small>F</small> you have any half-brothers or -sisters or stepsisters or stepbrothers you have to remember that none of you chose to be born. Whatever arguments that come from having a different parent, you have to think that you didn't ask to be brought into the situation – it's your parents' issue and it's up to them to deal with it and protect you. You should never feel resentful, whether it be of your half-brother or stepsister, because what have they done wrong? In the same way, you didn't ask for any of it to happen, so don't take it out on each other.

You have to work hard at building up a relationship. So many great things can come from having lots of brothers and sisters so you should embrace them. I love the fact that I have Jessica and Louis in my life and that we're close – it makes my mum and dad really happy too. If your parents have made the decision to separate or get divorced, you have to make sure you find someone to talk to. It's going to be a really upsetting time and you have to make sure that someone listens to you and finds out what you want to do. Whatever you do, you must never sit in silence. What you think and feel is incredibly important. The Samaritans are always there to listen, but there are many other groups out there waiting to help:

Relate has over 600 centres in the UK that you can visit or alternatively call or email them for help and advice. You can get relationship support for you and your whole family if you're having a rough time. They offer different services including counselling, workshops and training courses. They offer support and advice if your parents are separating or divorcing, if you are having problems living with just one parent, or if you're having trouble getting on with your stepfamily.

They usually charge a fee but some centres do offer lower-cost counselling sessions. Call or go via the site to find your nearest centre.

☎ 0300 100 1234
www.relate.org.uk

Childline is also a brilliant and confidential phone line; calls are free so don't worry about them costing anything, and if you're ringing from a landline they won't even show up on the bill:

☎ 0800 1111
www.childline.org.uk

You can't pick your family so if you've got a fucked-up one, pick some really good friends. Have smart people in your life because you learn stuff from them.

DYSLEXIA

How do I know if I'm dyslexic and what do I do?

Dyslexia doesn't mean you're stupid. It doesn't mean you're really bloody clever either, which is what some people also think. What it means is you learn differently. If you're struggling with your reading, writing or spelling, the key thing is to make sure you see an expert who is able to diagnose it as early as possible. That way, you won't be held back in class.

The British Dyslexia Association offers lots of information for you and your parents, including hints and tips for school, how tutors can help, technology that can help you at school and work, support in finding work and even advice on taking your driving test.

> The British Dyslexia Association
> Unit 8, Bracknell Beeches
> Old Bracknell Lane
> Bracknell
> RG12 7BW
>
> ☎ 0845 251 9002
> ☎ 0845 251 9003
> 🖶 0845 251 9005
> ✎ helpline@bdadyslexia.org.uk
> www.bdadyslexia.org.uk

Need to know

This general-health site is really good for explaining what dyslexia is, what causes it and how to work out if you have it:

www.need2know.co.uk/health/health_services

Worried that you have dsylexia?

If you're worried that you may have dyslexia, **British Dyslexics** is the largest website on the subject in the world. I've visited this site loads of times and I can't recommend it enough. It understands everything you might be worried about and is even colour-coded so that it's easy to navigate. It's a registered charity too and it specialises in helping young people who are trying to adapt to being dyslexic.

The charity is run by dyslexics so they totally understand what it's like.
☎ 01352 716 656
www.dyslexia.uk.com

How to manage dyslexia

Over the years I've learned different ways to manage my dyslexia and it's enabled me to do live TV and present lots of programmes successfully. There is no reason why you shouldn't fulfil your dreams.

When I'm worried about reading out loud, I write what I want to say on individual index cards. It means I'm not so daunted by a massive chunk of copy. I put this into practice when I spoke to a whole bunch of experts on World Contraception Day.

Another tip I've found useful is writing things out myself, instead of reading someone else's writing. As I write, I make a mental note, which helps me remember it. It's a tried-and-tested plan for me.

Another charity that will be able to help you do your job and manage your dyslexia is Dyslexia Action. There are centres all over the country where you can go for advice and support – find your nearest centre on their site:

www.dyslexiaaction.org.uk

SOME people with dyslexia are unusually creative. It's common for artists and musicians to have dyslexia, and they're incredibly talented at what they do. It's funny how the brain compensates. Sometimes it helps if you can speak to other people about their dyslexia and how they live with it.

Famous dyslexics include:

Keira Knightley	Jamie Oliver
Will Smith	Tommy Hilfiger
Orlando Bloom	David Bailey
Keanu Reeves	Andy Warhol
Tom Cruise	John Lennon

Being Dyslexic is one of the largest dyslexia forums. It has thousands of members and you can chat to them. It's free and the site also includes an online self-test and lots of resources including study guides. The site also has blogs and a Facebook group.
www.beingdyslexic.co.uk

Books and events

Dyslexia: How to Survive and Succeed at Work by Sylvia Moody, Vermillion, £9.99, ISBN 978-0091907082
This is a brilliant book for dyslexics who have problems at work, such as with reading, writing, organisation, time management and remembering things.

Dyslexia: A Teenager's Guide by Sylvia Moody, Vermillion, £9.99, ISBN 978-0091900014
This offers tips on reading, writing, spelling, remembering things, taking notes, studying and dealing with exams.

To celebrate Dyslexia Week, the British Dyslexia Association has launched a Wake Up 2 Dyslexia national campaign which runs for a month each year. The main aim is to raise money and awareness about dyslexia. Get in touch via the the British Dyslexia Association for more information.

ADHD & BULLYING

THERE is nothing embarrassing about being diagnosed with ADHD.
Here's a good fact: children who are diagnosed with ADHD often
have above-average intelligence. They just find it hard to channel their
concentration on one task.

You should take a look at ADDISS, the National Attention Deficit
Disorder Information and Support Service.

This charity will really sort you out and it can offer information and
advice about ADHD for you, your family and even your teachers. You can
call, email or visit their resource centre, where they have lots of books and
videos on ADHD. They also have information on Tourette's Syndrome and
Asperger's Syndrome if you need advice or help with this.

> ADDISS Resource Centre
> 2nd Floor, Premier House
> 112 Station Road
> Edgware
> HA8 7BJ
>
> ☎ 020 8952 2800
> ✆ info@addiss.co.uk
> www.addiss.co.uk

Misunderstood

DOCTORS think that ADHD is caused by a chemical imbalance in the brain
that affects the bit that controls attention, concentration and impulsivity.
There are lots of people out there to talk to about it who will help make
sense of how you're feeling.

Misunderstood is a charity that provides a helpline for you and your
family if you are affected by ADHD. They are helping to fund research
into treatments and finding ways to help kids deal with and manage their
ADHD, and they have a specialist ADHD consultant on site. They also

Fierce

hold lots of fundraising events during the year, to help raise money and awareness, so check out their site for further details.

☎ 01634 328 162
www.misunderstood.org.uk

THE only reason people bully is because they're fucking afraid. They're really afraid.

People say, 'Oh, just ignore them.' But you can't ignore them. The memories of what people say to you can actually torture you for ages afterwards – if you let them.

Over the years, I've learned to deal with people who are being horrible to me.

If someone doesn't like me, I go up to them and I say, 'What is your problem? What is your reason for not liking me?'

Back in the day they might have said, 'Because you're fat and you're stupid.'

I'd say back, 'That's not a good enough reason for you not to like someone. I'll see you later.' That usually makes them feel so bloody small.

In the past I've had, 'Because you're ugly.'

I'd say, 'That's OK, there are enough people in my life who don't think I'm ugly.'

It's just finding that confidence to cope with those bullies. You're always going to go through life with people saying things to you that you might not like. Dealing with a bully is about knowing how to handle yourself. Do you think at forty when someone says something to you that you don't like, you're going to stand back and take it? No, you won't. So, just remember bullies are the weaker people, that's why they're bullies. If you show maturity, you'll always come off the better person. A valuable lesson I've learned is that you can't go through life expecting everyone to love you all the time. You'd be very ignorant to think that could happen, so accept it's a big world. Some people will really love you, others won't. It's not your fault.

A great place to start for advice with bullying is the helpline **Youth2Youth**. It's the UK's first National Young Person's helpline, run by young people, for young people. Everyone is specially trained and they offer emotional support for 11–19 year olds. They are a great organisation if you don't want to talk to friends or family. Contact is by telephone, email via the site or online chat and is totally confidential.

You can also volunteer to help out – volunteers must be aged 16–21 and are carefully selected and trained so that they can help callers with a range of problems. Check out their website for the next training weekend.

☎ 020 8896 3675
(every Monday and Thursday evening from 6.30 p.m. to 9.30 p.m.)
www.youth2youth.co.uk

Famous people who were bullied at school

Gok Wan
David and Victoria Beckham
Barack Obama
Will Young
Rihanna
Jonathan Ross
Jamie Redknapp
Jessica Alba

Get Connected offer a free, confidential helpline. They can put you in touch with somewhere safe to stay for the night, offer advice or even just a shoulder to cry on. Contact them by telephone, email or webchat.

☎ 0808 808 4994
✆ help@getconnected.org.uk
www.getconnected.org.uk/home

Bullying UK is an award-winning charity which provides information and advice on bullying. They run workshops, speak at conferences and work with schools, youth organisations, the police and health trusts. Contact them via email, check out their site or Twitter.

✆ help@bullying.co.uk
www.bullying.co.uk

I'VE been a victim of people being mean about me on the internet and it isn't nice. Being in the public eye has meant that I've had to get used to people writing blogs about me that are not always flattering. But one thing I have learned is that with the introduction of Facebook and Twitter, we're all susceptible to things being written about us that we don't like. I do use Facebook and when I started dating my boyfriend, Luke Worrall, all sorts of girls were writing mean things about me on his page. That hurt.

What is cyberbullying? This is when someone uses technology, e.g. the internet or a mobile phone to deliberately hurt, humiliate, harass, intimidate or threaten someone else.

Examples include:

1. Sending nasty or threatening texts or emails.
2. Posting abusive messages online – on a social networking site, in a chatroom, or using IM.
3. Posting humiliating videos or pictures online, or sending them on to other people.
4. Taking on someone else's identity online in order to upset them.
5. Bad-mouthing and spreading rumours.
6. Setting up a hate site or a hate group on a social-networking site.
7. Prank calling, prank texts and messages.

Some cyberbullying is done just for a laugh or cheap joke, but that doesn't make it any less painful for the recipient. According to the CyberMentors website there is growing evidence that many young people don't take being online that seriously and hide behind anonymous profiles.

In 2007, YouTube introduced the first anti-bullying channel for youth, Beatbullying, engaging the assistance of celebrities to tackle the problem. They are on Bebo, MySpace and Flickr, and have a Facebook group.

Beatbullying is the UK's leading bullying-prevention charity – their aim is to work towards 'a world where bullying and child-on-child violence are unacceptable'.

CyberMentors is a part of a new Beatbullying initiative. It's the first peer-mentoring social-networking site run by young people to help and assist their peers both off and online.

CyberMentors	☎ 020 8771 3377
Beatbullying	✆ info@beatbullying.org
Units 1 + 4	www.cybermentors.org.uk
Belvedere Road	www.beatbullying.org
London	
SE19 2AT	

BEAUTY

I MET Neil Young when I was doing my second series of *Project Catwalk*. My make-up artist accidentally fell off the stage so Neil, who was head of the make-up team backstage, stepped in. He has been a make-up artist for seventeen years and is unbelievably talented. As well as doing my make-up, he works with the MAC team and is responsible for some of the most innovative make-up styles you'll see on the catwalks during each season's fashion week. He has done make-up for Shirley Bassey, Grace Jones, Helen Mirren – everyone! As well as being great at his job, he has also become a very good friend. When you're filming all day or on a long shoot, Neil always makes everyone laugh, which is exactly what you need.

Y OU should never leave the house – even in December – without wearing a high factor (and we're talking factor 30) on your face. It's so important and will prevent sun damage (sun in the winter can be just as harmful to your skin).

Don't smoke.

Use face wipes to remove make-up and cleanse your face every morning and evening (they don't have to be some fancy, expensive brand).

Moisturise, moisturise, moisturise. A skin care regime doesn't have to be complicated, and you don't have to use expensive products. The most important thing is that your skin needs to be hydrated. If your skin is not moisturised enough, there is no point in putting on make-up.

Neil says: Study your face

WHEN you're thinking about make-up, you shouldn't just think about the face. You should also think about the hair, the outfit and the accessories. If your clothes are busy, then keep the make-up simple. If you're wearing a simple black dress, you might want be more adventurous with your make-up. Also think about the occasion: Make-up should be fun and playful. If you're wearing a fifties-inspired outfit, sweep over a little red lipstick and a flick of black eyeliner for the ultimate statement.

Really study your bare face in the mirror and examine what you have to work with. Don't think about what you haven't got – think about what features are your strongest and play them up. Don't mask your face with make-up, think of enhancing instead. It's important to understand your face, eye and lip shape so that you can enhance them in the best way. The most wonderful thing about make-up is its ability not only to transform you physically but more importantly the way you feel about yourself. It's instant magic! Try not to do the same make-up every day so that it doesn't become a security mask. Celebrate what's great about your natural beauty and embrace it!.

Never over-tweeze your brows – they are so important for structuring the face. An over-tweezed brow is really ageing because what it suggests is that the hair is thinning. Full brows look so much more youthful. Go to a brow bar and get them done professionally. Always go on recommendation – if the person doing your brows hasn't got a nice shape themselves, don't let them do yours.

Kelly's top tip

ALWAYS carry a little tub of Vaseline around with you. You can use it as eyeshadow, to stop chapped lips and if your shoes are rubbing, add a little bit inside your shoes and it will stop straight away.

Neil's advice on stocking your make-up bag

START with a good moisturiser to hydrate the skin and a great foundation if you feel your skin needs evening out. Most skin needs foundation only down the centre of the face so apply sparingly and blend out towards the ears. Always seek professional advice when you're matching a foundation. All the major brands have a make-up artist working for them in big department stores. They will advise you on the best shade for your skin. The biggest mistake people make when buying a foundation is using it to make them darker, like a fake tan. A foundation should be used to even out your skin and help make it look flawless. It has to look like your skin in a bottle. There is no point in testing out the colour on the back of your hand. Where do you wear foundation? On your face – so that's where you should test it.

Don't spend a fortune on mascara – so long as you apply mascara in light coats from root to tip, allowing each coat to dry, you can achieve full voluminous lashes with any brand. Always remember to coat the back of the lashes as well as the front so that you coat the lash 360 degrees!

As a self-taught make-up artist I believe anyone can wear any colour around their eyes. It's all about the texture you choose and how much of the colour you see that makes all the difference. A bright blue on the eyes may look great on the catwalk but may look overpowering for an everyday look so opt for a cobalt-blue eyeliner instead – remember less is more and you can always add extra should you feel more confident – it's much more difficult to take away.

Wearing lip colour is about confidence – red or fuscia lips can make you feel instantly sexy, like putting on a pair of heels, but never let the lipstick wear you. If your lips are thin try medium to light tones in satin or gloss to plump them out. If you have very full lips and want to play them down opt for medium to dark tones in satin or matt – this will help to minimize. If you can't get a lip pencil to match your lipstick, go without. Lips look ultra modern when left undefined. If your lipstick bleeds MAC's Prep and Prime lip is great for keeping the colour firmly in place.

Lino Carbosiero – Hairdresser

Lino is really well-respected, so I went to visit him to get his top tips:

Hair do's:

1 Find a good hairdresser and build up a relationship with them. Make
them your friend. It's always good to go on recommendation from
your family and friends. A good hairdresser will always give a free
consultation.

2 Have a regular haircut (take advice on how often from your hairdresser),
but it should be anything from every six to twelve weeks.

3 Moisturise your hair. If you had a dry patch on your skin, you wouldn't
think twice about moisturising it. You should do the same for your hair
if the ends are dry. Having it cut regularly is a start, but you should also
put a treatment on it. You don't have to spend a fortune – you can go to
any high-street store like Boots or Superdrug and buy a conditioning
treatment. Depending on how damaged your hair is, you should moisturise
as little as once a month or as much as once a week.

4 Make your hair a joint venture – tell your hairdresser your ideas, but listen
to their thoughts too. Kelly and I have always worked together on all of her
hairstyles. Take a photograph; if you see the sides of a hairstyle you like
in one picture, and then maybe the back in another, cut them all out and
take them to your hairdresser. They will be able to tell you straight away
whether they can make the style work for you.

5 Always wear a hat if you're sunbathing to protect your hair. If you don't
want to wear a hat, buy a protective hair mask and leave it on while
you're in the sun. If you damage your hair in the sun, go straight to the
hairdresser and get the ends cut off. Hair is made of protein; therefore,
if you've stripped it off through sun damage, you need to put the protein
back in – this means using a good moisturiser every week until it gets
healthier and stronger.

Hair don'ts:

1 Don't overuse straightening irons. They are a great invention (I wish I'd thought of them, so I'm not telling you to stop using them) – just don't use them too often as they make your hair very brittle. Use them once a week, put a protective serum on beforehand and don't hold them on the same strand of hair – keep them moving up and down the hair.

2 If you want to dye your hair, save up and get it done professionally. It might take you weeks or months to save, but in the long-term you will be so grateful you did.

3 The biggest mistake people make is to use a home bleaching kit. There should be a warning on the bottle saying 'You will go orange'. I remember a mother brought her teenage daughter to me after she'd used a home bleaching kit and her hair was orange. It took us a whole year to grow it out.

4 Don't cut your hair off if you're having a bad day, your boyfriend's dumped you or you hate your job... don't do it! Think about it first. You will always regret having a drastic haircut on a whim.

5 If you have a long face, don't have a style that drags your face down. Have a fringe or layers done around the face to bring it up.

6 If you have a round face, don't emphasise the jaw line – it will only make your face look rounder.

Advice

Neil's final tips

L OOK after your make-up. Invest in an alcohol spray and use it to clean your lipstick. Lots of germs and infections can be spread from using your lipstick over and over again, so you need to look after it properly.

Never be afraid of make-up. It's not a tattoo. It comes off.

It's important to update your make-up products. You can always spot women who wore black eyeliner in their twenties and are still doing it in their fifties. You can go to a professional counter and get updated – let them show you the latest techniques and products. Invest in some good professional brushes that will help you acheive your chosen look easily and will look after you!

SEX

HAVING sex for the first time is not something that should be taken lightly. Speaking from experience, the first time I had sex I really wasn't ready. I thought I was being grown up, but I'd not thought about all the emotions that went with it.

My mum has always been honest with me about sex, but not everybody has a mum like mine! If you feel you haven't got that sort of relationship with your mum and dad, that's fine too because there are lots of organisations out there who are able to offer advice. You should never feel too embarrassed to ask for help.

If you're thinking about having sex for the first time, you need to get the right advice on contraception. A good place to start – and the right place – is **fpa** (Family Planning Association). It's their job to give the best advice so don't feel self-conscious. Their website – as well as their phone lines – offer advice on a wide range of issues from contraception, common sexually transmitted infections, pregnancy choices and abortion to planning a pregnancy. They also provide details of clinics, plus sexual-assault referral centres. You can ring the helpline or read their range of leaflets, which are specifically designed for young people.

> Sexual Health Direct is open Monday – Friday, 9 a.m. – 6 p.m.
> ☎ 0845 122 8690
> www.fpa.org.uk
> To find your nearest clinic: www.fpa.org.uk/Findaclinic

Make the right decision

If you need to talk to someone, ring the Sexwise Helpline where they will put you through to a specially trained advisor in your area.

☎ 0800 282 930 between 7 a.m. and midnight, seven days a week
www.maketherightdecision.co.uk/html/
clinics

Sex Etc

This is sex advice written by teenagers aimed at their peers, covering everything from deciding when to have sex for the first time and emotional health to birth control, STIs and abortion. You can ask their experts for confidential advice, view videos about sexual health, follow the blog which deals with all the latest topics, and enter forums in which teens discuss everything and anything sex-related.

www.sexetc.org

G IRLS – and boys – you need to protect yourselves against infection and unwanted pregnancy.

I go three, maybe four times a year to get tested for sexually transmitted infections. Most of the time I don't even need to, but I just go for peace of mind, even when I'm in a trusting, long-term relationship. It's just good to be body-aware.

RUThinking is a really useful site that gives advice to girls and boys on loads of topics including emergency contraception, STIs, smear tests, your body, your sexuality, peer pressure and finding local clinics. Don't forget you can buy emergency contraception over the counter in most pharmacies. You need to be over sixteen and it will cost around twenty pounds. The pharmacist will ask you some questions, but don't be put off – it's just to ensure the medication is safe for you to take.

☎ 0800 282 930
www.ruthinking.co.uk

Fierce

I WAS the global ambassador for World Contraception Day in 2008. This is a global annual event that happens every year on 26 September. The aim is to help and encourage young people to make informed decisions about their sex life. Check out their website – it's really good.

www.your-life.com
www.mariestopes.org.uk

ALCOHOL

As the child of someone who has an addiction – and it can be any addiction, not just alcohol – you've got to realise that you can't be expected to go through it alone.

You have to get support. If there isn't anyone in your family who you can speak to then you have to look outside. There are many organisations who are there to give you advice and support and you should **NEVER** be afraid to seek their help.

When you hear people say AA, they are referring to Alcoholics Anonymous. They have literally saved the lives of millions of people all over the world.

Alcoholics Anonymous
PO Box 1
10 Toft Green
York
YO1 7ND

☎ 01904 644 026
☎ National helpline no:
0845 769 7555
✆ help@alcoholics-anonymous.org.uk
www.alcoholics-anonymous.org.uk

If you go online, there is a starter pack. You can also read the stories of other members, which will help you realise there is support and that you're not on your own.

AA is completely confidential and the meetings are ninety-minutes long.

IF a member of your family or a close friend is an alcoholic you need to remember that as well as being a support to them, you might need a bit of support too. There is a great organisation called Al-Anon Family Groups, which offers support for the families and friends of someone who is suffering from alcoholism. Even if the person in your life has stopped drinking, but you're still affected by it, you can contact them for help. Their details are below. If you're in this situation, do contact them because their help is truly invaluable.

Al-Anon Family Groups UK & Eire
61 Great Dover Street
London
SE1 4YF

☎ 020 7403 0888
Open 10 a.m. – 10 p.m. every day
✆ enquiries@al-anonuk.org.uk
www.al-anonuk.org.uk

If you can't face walking into a room of strangers, you can also go to the online advice group: Dry Out Now. They will be able to give you all the advice you need on the web so it means you won't feel scared or self-conscious. There will be so many services in your area that, when you feel ready, you'll be able to visit or talk. This site will be able to give you all of those details. It also offers advice on an alcohol detox at home.

☎ 0845 370 0203
✆ freeadvice@dryoutnow.com
www.dryoutnow.com

VICODIN

IT'S not easy having a parent who has an addiction. It's always important to find someone in your life who you can talk honestly to without feeling scared. We were lucky that we had our mum and she was always incredibly honest. If you're not in a position to talk to your mum or dad, find another adult who will be able to make the time to talk to you. It really helps.

Another good reason for finding a person you trust to talk to is that it stops you from being resentful. At times I have felt resentment, but one of the best pieces of advice I have been given was 'you have to let go'. In the end, the only person who it's hurting is you. That doesn't help anyone.

Just because you think you're hiding something doesn't mean no one has noticed. Even if you've fooled your mum and dad, your little sister or your older brother might have worked out something's up. If you're ready to talk, your brothers and sisters – or good friends – are sometimes better than parents.

⋆

DRUGS can ruin the best friendships. Jack and I had been incredibly close up until the day we both started to take drugs. When we took drugs we started to hate each other. To me, Jack's perfect. He's such a gentleman, funny and so, so smart. But for two years we fought terribly because we were both taking drugs.

ADDACTION is a brilliant charity that offers confidential help to under eighteens with their Young Addaction services – get in touch to find your nearest centre.

They also understand that you might be affected by the drug abuse of someone in your family, and the massive emotional, and often financial, impact this can have – their family support service is fantastic.

Addaction
67–69 Cowcross Street
London
EC1M 6PU
☎ 020 7251 5860
www.addaction.org.uk

For families:
Adfam
25 Corsham Street
London
N1 6DR
☎ 020 7553 7640
✉ admin@adfam.org.uk
www.adfam.org.uk

How did Vicodin make me feel?

IT made me feel like a totally different person. I'd lived in the UK and been very comfortable with myself and who I was but then I moved to America, where everyone kept telling me I was weird, just because I spoke with a different accent, and I'd started to believe it. Over the months all my confidence disappeared but Vicodin was confidence in a bottle. It made me feel amazing.

F RANK is an amazing website, packed with information. There is a really great A–Z of drugs, which has lots of details on the street names for substances, what they look like, the effects, the chances of getting hooked, cost, the law, purity, the risks and the chemical reactions, so you know all the facts.

They also cover everything from how to cope at festivals, peer pressure, the effects on your body, comedowns, whiteys, bad experiences; you can also upload poems, postcards and artwork that you have created to the 'your space' area. There is a cannabis self-help course – take the online course which will help you stop or cut down using cannabis. After the initial five steps, you are signed up for the whole thing, which is all online and completely confidential.

You can email them via the site, call free 24 hours a day, and you can even talk to Frank in 120 languages as they have interpreters ready to help.

☎ 0800 77 66 00
www.talktofrank.com

A s I've said, you can become addicted to anything – it was Vicodin for me, but it might be something totally different that at first seems to be your magic remedy. Find out as much as you can about the things that people are offering you – sometimes knowing what that magic potion is made from can be enough to change your mind, whether it's formaldehyde in cigarettes or battery acid in ecstasy.

EATING ISSUES

I DON'T care what anyone says, we all like to eat shit food. There is absolutely nothing wrong with treating ourselves. But our bodies work better when we have a balanced diet. The Food Standards Agency – Eat Well campaign is really good at offering advice on the sort of foods we should and shouldn't be eating. I don't know about you, but it's only something I've been clued up about in my twenties. I didn't think about it in my teens – I wish I had. It also explains food labels and what it all means. They can be bloody confusing.

It has advice on how to get enough iron, advice on spots, how to boost your energy levels and how to choose healthy snacks.

www.eatwell.gov.uk

W EIGHT is something we all think about, but it doesn't have to be a huge problem. I found, especially when I became a teenager, that everyone in my class had some sort of anxiety about their weight at some stage. Check out Teen Weight Wise. It's good because it offers lots of practical tips to help you manage your weight, plus lots of information on nutrition and maintaining a healthy lifestyle.

www.teenweightwise.com

ANOREXIA and bulimia are common illnesses – and they are illnesses – if you're a sufferer, you need to get help. Beat is a charity that will give you the advice you need to get better. If you're feeling worried or embarrassed, they can help you on the phone or will email and put you in touch with someone in your area. They also have message boards and forums where you can chat to other people.

☎ 0845 634 1414
Text: 07786 201 820
🖰 fyp@b-eat.co.uk
www.b-eat.co.uk

✧

SOMETIMES just being able to read about different conditions can help you realise that you might be suffering from an eating disorder. Eating Disorder Expert has lots of articles that you'll find really interesting. They deal with a range of subjects from binge-eating, compulsive exercising and weird eating habits. It also highlights the side-effects you get from purging and starving yourself.

www.eatingdisorderexpert.co.uk

CANCER

WHEN my mum was diagnosed with cancer it was a terrible shock. I'm not going to lie to you. But there are so many different things you can do to help make the situation more comfortable.

Instead of looking at how difficult things are, look at what you do have – someone in your life who you love and who you should try and spend as much time with as possible. Little things like sitting together and watching a movie are so very important or just sitting quietly and enjoying each other's company. Mum and I would sit and chat for hours about nothing in particular.

When someone is sick they don't need someone telling them what to do or pandering to them. You need to make them laugh. They need someone who is normal around them who tries to take their mind off the fact that they're ill.

Sadly, cancer is something that will probably affect nearly all of us at some point in our lives whether it's a family member, a friend, a colleague or if we suffer from the illness ourselves. But there are so many fantastic charities and organisations that do a great job of supporting cancer sufferers and their families and friends. One of those is Cancer Research UK. It is the leading funder of cancer research in the UK. You can call their specialist nurses Monday to Friday, between 9 a.m. and 5 p.m. You can also give something back and volunteer or even enter a Race for Life to help raise money for this amazing charity.

Cancer Research UK
PO Box 123
Lincoln's Inn Fields
London
WC2A 3PX

☎ (supporter Services) 020 7121 6699
☎ (switchboard) 020 7242 0200
Freephone: 0808 800 4040
www.cancerresearchuk.org

SOMETHING you'll learn very quickly when a member of your family has cancer is who your real friends are. Some people are, sadly, only there for the good times. But you'll find people who are always there for you too, which is so important. Elton John and his partner David Furnish were always there for us when my mum got cancer and there'll be people in your life who're there for you too.

You can also turn to Macmillan for emotional and practical support. You might find also find strength in talking to other people in similar situations, and sharing stories on the online forums. It really will help you feel better.

Macmillan also offer help if you are having financial problems as a result of cancer.

Macmillan Cancer Support
89 Albert Embankment
London
SE1 7UQ
☎ 020 7840 7840
www.macmillan.org.uk

I ALWAYS give my support to the Teenage Cancer Trust. This charity does a really great job of improving the lives of teenagers and young adults with cancer. They do all sorts of things to raise money and awareness and I've been involved in doing pictures for T-Shirts. But they do also have a whole bunch of great things going on like organising concerts and events.

Teenage Cancer Trust   ✆ 020 7612 0370
3rd floor   ☎ tct@teenagecancertrust.org
93 Newman Street   www.teenagecancertrust.org
London
W1T 3EZ

Fierce

Another organisation that is there for teenagers is TIC, Teen Info on Cancer. It is a brilliant resource that you can go to for support and advice in order to help you deal with the totally understandable fear of cancer.

It also provides a place for teenagers with cancer to go to, build a community and help each other.

www.click4tic.org.uk

DRUGS

VICODIN is an opiate like heroin and, in the wrong hands, it can be really addictive. It depresses the nervous system and relieves pain. If you abuse this painkiller, like I was starting to, it makes you feel really lethargic and woozy-headed, like you're not really living life. Physically you're there, but your brain is in another place. The effects of one tablet last anything from six to twelve hours. The guy who gave me the first tablet had found someone who could get a bigger supply from a contact he'd made at a pharmaceutical company in Los Angeles, so I was paying him about £600 for a bottle of three hundred tablets.

WHEN I was taking Vicodin everyone hated me. They hated me because of the way the tablets made me feel and behave. Those tablets made me miserable, angry and hateful. Everyone hated me. My mum and dad hated me, my brother hated me and the people I worked with hated me. No one wanted to work with me. That makes you feel terrible about yourself and now, yes, very ashamed. That's what drugs do.

The amazing thing about the help out there is that there are people who are committed to getting you through everything. Some organisations can help you find the strength to fight your addiction and others are brilliant at helping you cope with it before you're ready to take it on.

Fierce

Turning Point are a fantastic charity that are highly experienced in dealing with people with drug problems. They tailor their service to suit each person and aim to make your life happier, whether it's coping with the addiction, helping to keep your family together, or finding a new job.

Standon House
21 Mansell Street
London
E1 8AA

☎ 020 7481 7600
✆ info@turning-point.co.uk
www.turning-point.co.uk

Narconon

Narconon has helped thousands of people get to grips with their drug addiction. There are over 190 rehab centres around the world so check out the website to find your nearest centre. Counsellors are available twenty-four hours a day, seven days a week.

When you decide you're ready to tackle your addiction don't do what I did and try to beat it on your own. There's amazing help out there – make sure you use it. I've already mentioned a couple of great organisations but there are others. Narconon is a good place to start if you're not sure who best to speak to.

Narconon UK
Caple Ne Ferne
2 Albany Road
St Leonards on Sea
East Sussex
TN38 0LN
☎ 0800 169 4803
www.drugrehab.co.uk

REHAB

I F you've been a heavy user, you can actually die if you don't receive the correct medical attention to come off drugs. Your body can quite simply go into shock. It needs to find a way to function again without all these crazy chemicals.

If you're thinking about attempting to withdraw from a drug addiction get in touch with an organisation like UK Rehab.

UK-Rehab is a non-profit-making organisation that gives free information on all things drug-related. The site is totally impartial and offers a drug rehab directory showing where to get help and explains exactly what kind of help is on offer. There is also an online guest book and addiction blog; real-life stories so you are not alone.

UK-Rehab.com   ☎ 01202 318072
26 Hampshire Court   ✆ admin@uk-rehab.com
Bourne Avenue   www.uk-rehab.com
Bournemouth
BH2 6DW

A NYONE who thinks taking drugs is glamorous should experience what it's like to withdraw, it's the worst pain you'll probably ever go through. It really is.

DIFFERENT sorts of rehab facilities work for different people and some can be really expensive. If money is an issue, then this great site – Addiction Advisor – will help you find the lowest treatment costs available, including residential programmes where you can stay over. They offer free addiction advice via email and have a self-assessment service online to help you work out what to do, in addition to details of all the UK treatment centres.

☎ 0845 003 8908
www.addictionadvisor.co.uk

THE best thing to do in rehab is to shut up and listen. Your best thinking got you there, now you need to listen to someone else's better thinking and advice.

Rehab is not glamorous. It's not a vacation without alcohol. You feel shit from the minute you walk in, to the minute you leave. And when you do leave, you're experiencing the worse fear ever because you don't know whether you're going to stick to the programme or relapse.

The way that I look at it is someone who is buying crack off the street is no worse than the person who is being prescribed it by their doctor. Drugs don't discriminate. An addict is an addict. An addiction is an addiction.

Advice

THE MUSIC INDUSTRY

THERE are few people who know more about having a successful music career than Louis Walsh. My audition for Chicago was terrifying, but I know there are things you can do to make sure they go well, so I asked Louis for his top audition tips and his essential do's and don'ts for making that crucial first impression.

Always remember auditions are basically job interviews for performers. And, like every interview, you will only succeed in getting the job if you are right for it.

Louis' top tips for making the most of your audition:

Look confident: Introduce yourself and speak clearly and confidently, even if you don't feel it. Wear a smile. Look as if you're enjoying yourself and not as if you're in front of a firing squad. An audition is about looking for stars, not timid church mice.

Pick the right songs: Select two songs that you love, that you're comfortable with and that show off your voice. Find a song that's a bit unusual or take in a classic song and put your individual stamp on it.

Get to the best part first: Less is definitely more. You might have just seconds before they call 'next', so make sure those seconds count.

Don't make excuses: Don't apologise in advance of your audition. No one wants to hear that they're about to listen to a bad audition because you've got a sore throat, blocked sinuses or you were up all night. Just get on with it.

Fierce

Know your song: Know the words of the song or songs that you want to perform inside out. Nerves won't wash. If you can't handle the pressure of a small audition, how do you expect to handle a live audience? The only time you should read lyrics or music is if you are given something specific to perform. Even then, make sure you look up and let the judges see you sing. If possible, find out in advance whether you will be singing with a pianist, a capella or if it's ok to bring a backing track.

Look smart and look the part: Image is hugely important in the world of showbusiness yet incredibly many turn up for auditions looking like disinterested slobs. If you can't be bothered, how do you expect anyone else to take you seriously? Be warned, this is not an invitation to arrive looking like a complete plonker from a bad rap video. Lose the shades, the bling and the attitude.

Should you even be there? Don't waste people's time. Make sure you fit the criteria for the audition you are attending. The one thing no one can really help you with is a genuine singing voice. It still amazes me how many people come to auditions who haven't a note in their head. If that's you accept that a career as a singer might not be for you and move on.

Do: Keep calm as you walk into the audition room. Try slow, deep breaths, positive thinking, or whatever it takes to keep yourself feeling relaxed. Remember – the judges are human too.

Don't: Try to be someone you're not, as this will only make you more nervous. Don't dress up as the person you are singing as it implies that you don't have a personality of your own. If you really do want to use props, keep them to a minimum – at the end of the day, the judges want to see you and hear your voice.

Do: Have something to say about yourself so you can be memorable; the judges will remember those who have made them smile, laugh or cry.

Don't: Don't get cocky, talk too much or be over-confident; you have to get the right mix of showing respect to the judges, but at the same time selling yourself.

Do: Try to introduce yourself to the team when you arrive or before you audition. Make sure you tell them why you're there and if you have an interesting story as they may want to film it.

Don't: Blend in with the crowd; choose a song that means something to you, but nothing too quirky. However, if auditioning for a musical role, you should know the most famous song from the production as the judges will probably ask you to sing it.

Do: Try to act as well as sing: use emotions and movement as this is much more interesting for both you and the judges, plus it shows you have a range of talents.

Don't: Go outside your comfort zone. Steer clear of songs by divas such Aretha Franklin, Mariah Carey, Whitney Houston and Christina Aguilera. I know from personal experience how hard it is to stay awake through countless bad versions if 'I Will Always Love You', 'The Greatest Love of All' and 'Flying Without Wings'.

Do: Bring someone with you; there's a lot of waiting around involved.

Don't: Take it personally: If you are turned down, accept that you are simply not the right person for that particular job at that particular time. It doesn't mean you're not talented or you don't have a future in the music industry. Get over it and try again. You may do fifty auditions and get nowhere because the competition is fierce. Look on every audition as a learning experience that gives you more practice in performing live.

FASHION

IFIRST met Brooke Dulien, who is based in LA, when I launched my music career, and we've been really good friends ever since. Brooke totally gets my style and we make a great team. As well as being a stylist, Brooke is also a jewellery designer with her own jewellery line, White Trash Charms, and has worked with some of the best people in the business including Anastasia, Janet Jackson, Gwen Stefani and Jessica Simpson. Since she gives such fantastic advice, I've picked her brains so that you can share her top five style tips:

Use the eighty/twenty rule like Kelly.

Always keep eighty per cent of your wardrobe streamlined and simple with a fantastic fit. You can play with the other twenty per cent by using bolder accessories, mixing decades or bringing in another colour or a killer handbag.

Take a picture.

You know the saying 'take a picture, it lasts longer'? Well, if you're not sure about your outfit, take a picture – that way you will know right away if you need to delete something in your wardrobe before you head out the door. Perspective like this is really simple way to get affirmation on your look, plus it will show you if the outfit is see-through! So take a quick snap with your phone camera – I promise this will stop many future fashion mistakes before they happen.

Create a mini-wardrobe kit.

You never know if a button is going to pop or your zip fail! Every girl needs a proper wardrobe kit for a last-minute emergency. Quick-fix musts to include in the kit are: safety pins, baby wipes (the best for removing makeup from clothes), double-sided tape (makes instant hems, holds a T-shirt in place, keeps a bra from slipping off your shoulders etc.), mini-lint brush, and a tiny sewing kit with an array of threads.

Don't forget to be versatile with your wardrobe!

One of the keys to a good wardrobe is being able to dress simple looks up or down. Have a drawer dedicated to wonderful socks and tights; this includes coloured or patterned tights. It's so easy to take a summer dress and make it work in winter – all you have to do is add tights and you have changed the entire look.

Never wear anything you don't feel good in.

Don't follow trends just because they are in magazines or your friends are wearing them. Remember – style is something that you create for yourself – you know yourself best. When you are confident, you wear it well, and that's true style.

I HAVE mixed feelings about going to London Fashion Week or any Fashion Week, come to think of it; I love going to see the new clothes and getting some idea of what I might be able to wear. I like to see the shows and make a mental note of how I'd like to accessorise a certain dress. But there is a downside too. There are always a million photographers in your face and there is such a hierarchy at every show. You'll see the pictures of all these famous people in a line looking like they're having a great time, but there has been so much going on behind the scenes to ensure that the right person is sitting in the right seat, next to the right person. You'd never find an influential editor sitting in the second row. That would never happen. And another thing I don't like is the way that everyone gossips about who the designer talked to after the show at the party. It's a class system for fashionistas and it's just ridiculous. At the end of the day, I'm just going along to see what I can buy from them. There is nothing glamorous about being a model. The grossest thing for me is looking at all the models' feet as they walk down the runway. Their feet are always covered in blisters and plasters because they've been wearing shoes that are the wrong size and none of them can walk properly. And I love it when they have cellulite. I think, 'Ha, you're just like the rest of us.' I tell you, more models have cellulite than not!

Top ten fashion tips:

1 Invest in Spanx. The right underwear can make an outfit. It can smooth your shape or hold you in all the right places. Big knickers are not embarrassing – they're a bloody life-saver! Don't follow the fashion trend of going knickerless and waving your fanny around. I think it's another form of addiction. It's an addiction to attention.

2 Always have a great pair of shoes in your wardrobe. Invest in an expensive pair. A good pair of heels. Shoes can make the outfit. You wear a pair of Chanel shoes – no one would ever think that the rest of your outfit isn't Chanel and that it might be from Primark. And actually, there is nothing wrong with Primark either.

3 I don't think you have to spend a lot of money on a bag. But pick one that shows off your personality. It's with you come rain or shine.

4   Invest in a good overcoat. You should always spend money on a coat because it will last for ever and a good coat will always be in for several seasons.

5   A great pair of jeans is really important. Find that one pair that you always feel good in. You can make jeans look fancy or you can make them look casual. For me, the cheaper the jeans, the better the fit. I get my jeans from Topshop and they only cost forty pounds.

6   It's important to have a great bra. If your bra doesn't fit, it can make you look fatter or saggy. Go to M&S or another underwear store and get professionally fitted.

7   Don't wear spaghetti straps if your arms are not toned. It's not a good look.

8   Avoid flesh-coloured tights. They're just so old-fashioned.

9   Look after your clothes. Hang them up properly. Take pride in them.

10 Don't squeeze your body into a size smaller just because you don't want to admit you're a twelve or a fourteen. Wear the correct size for your body shape. Squeezing into a pair of trousers that are a size too small will only make you have a muffin top.

Fierce

Notes

Advice

Notes

Fierce

Notes

Advice

Notes

Fierce

Notes

Advice

Notes